Running Against The Wind

"...factual and accurate...wonderful book." John J. Ryan, Executive Director, Police Athletic League

"I enjoyed reading Running Against the Wind...It reveals how the DeSaussure twin girls used the vehicle of the PAL to enter the wider world outside of Bed-Stuy..." Benjamin Ward, Commissioner (Ret.) New York City Police Department

Much love
Inge Auerbacher
4-22-01

Front cover art by Pamela Shanteau

W0010608

Other books by Inge Auerbacher

I Am A Star

Beyond the Yellow Star to America

RUNNING AGAINST THE WIND

The true story of twin sisters from Brooklyn who changed the lives of thousands of African-American youngsters in New York City.

by
Inge Auerbacher

Royal Fireworks Press
Unionville, New York

In loving memory of the Auerbacher and
DeSaussure parents, whose spirit and love for
humanity made ours a better world.
They taught us to be kind, and respect people of
every race, ethnicity and religion.
We thank God that we are their children.
We thank them for the most precious gifts of
open-mindedness and optimism.

Copyright © 2000, R Fireworks Publishing Co., Ltd.
All Rights Reserved.

Royal Fireworks Press, Inc.
1 First Avenue, PO Box 399
Unionville, NY 10988-0399
TEL: (845) 726-4444
FAX: (845) 726-3824
email: rfpress@frontiernet.net

ISBN: 0-88092-437-3

Printed in the United States of America using vegetable based inks on
acid-free, recycled paper by the Royal Fireworks Printing Co. of
Unionville, New York.

Author's Acknowledgements

I want to express my heartfelt gratitude to the extended DeSaussure clan for their warmth and kindness, permitting me to enter their lives and adopting me into their wonderful family.

I must thank the late composer James Donenfeld for the music entitled "Running Against the Wind." I treasure the many years of our collaboration in songwriting and will always hold dear his memory: gentle, caring, talented.

I am grateful to my publisher, Royal Fireworks Press, for believing in the project.

I am indebted to John J. Ryan, Executive Director, Police Athletic League; Benjamin Ward, Commissioner (Ret.) New York City Police; 1199, National Health and Human Service Employees Union, whose magazine article sparked the idea for this book; and to Margarita Corporan for her pictures of the 80th Anniversary celebration of the PAL in New York City.

Many thanks also to Anne Donenfeld, Florence Weinstein, Mary Louchheim, Allen Lee Sessoms, and Wayne Puff for their continuing inspiration and friendship.

Acknowledgements

Thank you to the most important men in our lives, second only to our father; Mr. William Jackson, Captain Vincent Kiernan, and Patrolman Americo Bacci. We hope that our story adequately represents your support, respect and love, and the influence you had on our lives.

Thank you also to Dr. Arthur Risbrook, former director of the Marcus Garvey Nursing Home; to Mr. Lloyd Curtis for being the brother we never had; and to Dr. Stewart Kessler, Chairman of the Department of Emergency Medicine, Elmhurst Hospital Center, for your generosity and leadership in our department as well as for coaching a Jersey Shore Little League club.

And thank you to Inge Auerbacher, author and friend for more than thirty years, for being a kind, loving and sincere human being, who reaches out to all of God's Children. We thank you for making our small part of history glow.

—Mary & Martha

Foreword

To critics who wonder why a Jewish white woman has written about the very devout, black Christian DeSaussure family, my answer is simply that I have had a 30-year friendship with Mary, empathize with discrimination, and believe that youngsters today should know about Mary's and her twin sister Martha's history-making strides. Their faith and determination to win races and go where no Black female runners had raced before, opened doors for young minority female athletes today.

I have experienced prejudice, having been sensitized to it by growing up in Nazi Europe amid the expanding venom and surviving the Holocaust in a concentration camp. I know well the feeling of a child's isolation and humiliation. And I applaud with all my heart the accomplishments of Mary and Martha.

When Mary's curiosity moved her to open the heavy door of the13th Regiment Armory in Brooklyn, New York, she set in motion a chain of events that would change the fate of her family, and thousands of New York's African-American children for years to come.

Inge Auerbacher

CHAPTER 1

In Brooklyn during the winter of 1945, the streets of Stuyvesant Heights (now called Bedford Stuyvesant) were a panoply of color and movement with Jews from Eastern Europe, Italians, Germans, African-Americans, Irish and other immigrants. Each group was low-income, but rich in its unique homeland culture. The American "melting-pot" swirled, and optimists, dreamers from outside the mix, chose to see the commotion as a blending pinwheel. But beneath the dreamer's view, beneath the coating of clean snow and bright winter coats and scarves, the stew pot simmered with the surfacing heat of racial problems.

The Allies were now making good headway in the war. At first, feelings of relief and euphoria affected everyone. Our victorious soldiers—fathers, brothers, uncles, even some aunts and sisters—would soon be welcomed home. The war had separated families. Now they would be whole again. It was time to resume life, a time to dream again and begin new ventures, a time to live for tomorrow, not just day by day. The war had shattered lives. Now the healing could begin. During the war, people of different cultures—but not different races—fought side by side to bring peace back to a war-torn world. Would the good feeling of patriotism linger and grow and allow the red, white and blue American Flag to wrap up the Black and White issues

1

that existed in America's urban areas and divided its people? Or, would the illusion of oneness dissipate?

New York City contained many ethnic groups, and many office buildings, many apartment houses, many stores and many private homes. Many of these doors were shut to Black Americans. As the return to peacetime living became a reality, old, established racial barriers again crystallized in the winter's cold.

Old locked doors leading to corridors of opportunity, better education and better jobs, had to be opened.

Hattie and Reverend William DeSaussure had lived in Stuyvesant Heights with their three young daughters, Willie and identical twins Mary and Martha, since the 1930's. But the family's roots reached back through South Carolina and the slave coast of West Africa.

Daddy was born in Eutaville, South Carolina. He received his preacher's license as a Baptist minister in 1924, and his Certificate of Ordination from the Samaritan Baptist Church in Varnsville, South Carolina in 1925. Mama's mother was a Native American of the Blackfoot Nation and her father was Black. Mama was born in Early Branch, South Carolina. She met Reverend DeSaussure, a widower, at a Baptist Convention, and they were married soon afterward.

They first set up home in Varnsville, where daughter Willie was born. Twins Mary and Martha were born

2

in Eutaville. Daddy's mother, a midwife, delivered the girls.

Daddy was of medium height, distinguished looking and definitely the boss of his family. He was dark-skinned, soft spoken and reserved. He had a will of iron. Mama was tall enough to be able to look Daddy in the eye, had a lighter complexion, and wore her hair pulled back in a small knot. Her priorities were her children and her family's home.

Home in Stuyvesant Heights was, at first, a four room, cold water railroad-flat apartment (One room followed the other in a straight line.) on the third floor of an attached brownstone building on Gates Avenue. Another family lived in the apartment below them, and a candy store was on the ground floor.

Several years later, the DeSaussures moved down the block to a first floor apartment in another brownstone row house. Two other Black families had apartments in the house. Mr. Asher, a religious Jewish gentleman, owned it.

Mr. Asher was warm-hearted, of medium stature and always wore a hat and a smile. He was known in the neighborhood as a street philosopher and friend, and never hesitated to give his opinion on family matters. He was a licensed plumber and did most of the repairs in his apartment house. But, when he ran into problems he would consult his friend, Mr. Rachel, another plumber who also always wore a hat. Mr. Rachel owned the house across the street. He was a stocky man. The heavy tools he carried drained his energy and droplets of sweat often ran down his face.

Mr. Asher really cared about the DeSaussure children and often made his thoughts about parenting in Stuyvesant Heights known: "Make sure your kids stay out of trouble...get them inside before dark...make sure they finish their homework because learning is important...and make sure they have nice friends." Mama smiled at his concern. She liked Mr. Asher.

Mr. Asher personally collected the rent the first of every month, and his visit was a pleasant event. Mama baked often. The aroma of her treats floated down the street and drew him like a magnet. He would stop in the hallway, before the door, and savor the sweet smells coming from the apartment.

As soon as he would knock on the door, Mama would invite him in. "Come right in, Mr. Asher, and have some of my freshly baked yeast rolls and pound cake. Would you like to join me in a cup of tea, or coffee?" she'd ask.

Following Mama into the dining room, Mr. Asher would answer, "All right Mrs. Desa, I'll sit for a minute or two."

Mr. Asher never said "DeSaussure," which he found too difficult to pronounce. He never stayed for just a minute or two. He always asked about the girls. When Daddy was home, the two men discussed current events and the Old Testament of the Bible. They were concerned about how the streets were getting a little

4

mean, how the war changed things. "The Mrs. and I are doing our best to keep them on the Lord's path," Daddy would reassure him.

Finally, after a bit more discussion, Mr. Asher would politely take his leave. "Time passes so quickly when we get to talking. I'd better be on my way," he'd say, getting up from the chair. "The tea and cake were delicious, Mrs. Desa. Be well."

On his way out the door, Mr. Asher would always shake Mama's and Daddy's hands, then climb up the hallway stairs to another apartment to collect the rent. Before closing her own door, Mama could hear him ringing the bell repeatedly, but no one answering. "That's too bad," she would say softly to herself as she walked to the kitchen to wash the few dishes, "he will have to come back another day and climb all those steps again."

Daddy organized the Goodwill Baptist Church in a store-front building just across the street from the apartment. His pastoral work was a labor of love, strictly voluntary. When the war broke out, he tried to enlist, but he was rejected because of his health. So, instead of soldiering, he worked as a machinist in the Brooklyn Navy Yard. After the war ended, he continued to work in a machine shop, and he took care of the maintenance of the apartment building in which the family lived. He went to school, too. He attended Boys High School and took night courses in advanced

5

mathematics. And he took a correspondence home-study Bible course.

Mama supplemented Daddy's small income with "day work," doing laundry and housekeeping in other people's homes three days of the week. Because she did not want to be far from her children, most of her clients were people from the neighborhood. Miss Sylvey, a middle-aged woman, was one of her favorites and a friend. Sometimes she would come to the house to see Mama and ask her to help her out. "Etta," she would say, "Passover is coming and I have to have the house really clean. You know that we can't even have one bread crumb around. I'm just not strong enough to do all the cleaning by myself any more." Mama would barely let her finish before saying, "Sure, Miss Sylvey, it's time for a spring cleaning anyway. I'll be glad to give you a hand."

Miss Sylvey always would give Mama a Passover gift of a box of matzos, a cracker-like unleavened bread, and say "Etta, this is for your family." On one occasion, Miss Sylvey introduced Mama to *gefilte fish,* strange elongated fish dumplings prepared from a variety of chopped fish. Mama liked the taste and asked for the recipe. The two women spent an afternoon preparing the fish and a horseradish dip, and Mama brought the food home. The dumplings were looked at for a long while before they were tasted, but one taste was all it took for Daddy to proclaim them a great success. Gefilte fish became a family favorite.

6

Mama always shared information about her clients' customs with her daughters. She explained Passsover to them. "Passover, the eight-day Jewish holiday, celebrates the exodus of the ancient Israelites from Egypt and slavery. It is a time when Jews eat only unleavened bread, *matzo*. This reminds them of their former bondage, and their escape. During the holiday, no regular bread is allowed in the house. Some vegetables are not allowed either. Miss Sylvey's home has to be clean as a whistle because she is a religious lady."

Mama made sure that on the days she worked the girls did not come home to an empty apartment. She arranged for them to go just across the street to the Cusinelli's, where they would do their homework with Anna and her younger sisters until Mama picked them up. The Cusinellis were an Italian-American family. Mrs. Cusinelli usually had an after-school snack ready for the children; often it was peanut butter and jelly sandwiches. The children delighted in letting large gobs of peanut butter melt in their mouths. And more often than not the words "Thank you…. You're so nice Mrs. Cusinelli, you make the best sandwiches," were muffled by the gooey, sweet mixture.

Mama had attended Mather's Boarding School on Lady's Island near Beaufort, South Carolina, when she was a girl. There she learned the art of smocking, needlepoint and quilt making. More than once it was said that Mama had gold in her hands. Now she taught

7

the skills to her daughters, and each of the beds in the apartment was covered with a beautiful, lovingly made quilt.

The success of her backyard Victory Garden led neighbors to say that Mama had a green thumb, too. During the war, the government encouraged people to grow vegetables in empty lots, Mama's plot was lush with flowers and food. She was proud of her immensely successful project. She grew collard greens, cucumbers, string beans, bell peppers, tomatoes and a blooming rainbow of flowers. Whatever she planted thrived. The vegetables helped to feed her family, and the flowers were shared with the members of the church. Mama's blossoms often adorned the church altar and made Sunday's service even more beautiful. "They are a gift from the Lord," she said.

The Victory Garden also brought forth another gift, a white female kitten, later named Flossie. While playing with the blossoms and the shadows in the garden, Flossie was so enticed by the aroma of Mama's cooking that she took the huge leap through the open kitchen window into the apartment, and into the hearts of the family.

Mama's father

Mama in the early 1930's on Market Street, Newark, N.J.

9

Mary and Martha at the World's Fair, 1939.

Kindergarten, PS 129, Brooklyn. Martha & Mary in plaid jackets and matching hats, front row center.

10

Above: Papa's Certificate of Ordination

Below: Papa's Preacher's License

11

Above: Mama in her victory garden, summer 1943

Below: Willie in the victory garden, summer 1943.

12

CHAPTER 2

The DeSaussure's apartment was comfortably furnished. There were a dining room and living room, a bedroom for the parents, and a bedroom for the girls. There were also a medium-sized eat-in kitchen and a small bathroom. Reflecting the spirit of the religious family, a picture of Christ hung on the living room wall. Mama kept the home spotless. Although Flossie was allowed to remain in the house, Daddy had set the rule that she was not to be on the beds...ever.

One day, Mama took the handmade quilts off the beds to wash them. She replaced the quilts with store-bought chenille bedspreads. Mama's beds were never unmade. One spread replaced the other on washdays. Within minutes of Mama walking out of the children's room, Flossie gracefully jumped up on the children's bed and fell asleep. Her snow-white body was almost indistinguishable from the chenille bedspread, and her rhythmic purring gently echoed in the otherwise silent room. Mary and Martha tiptoed into their room, hoping not to awaken the sleeping princess. Mary whispered to Martha, "If Daddy'd seen Flossie here, we'd really get it." Then she placed her finger to her lips signing Martha to keep very quiet. But Flossie felt the presence of the girls and opened her sleepy eyes. Instantly, the girls stroked the back and head of their best friend, and Flossie's tail moved slowly to show the girls that she was happy to see them. Flossie stretched, then twitched her pink nose. Suddenly, her triangle-shaped ears were erect and her golden eyes were peering at Martha's chest. She looked into Martha's eyes, threw a glance at Mary, and then jumped down off the bed and ran out of the room. The twins looked at each other and began to laugh. Flossie had locked on to the strange, pungent smell coming from Martha's Asefetida bag, which was attached by a small safety-pin to her undershirt, on her left side, under her dress. Instinctively, Mary felt for her own pouch and said, "What a silly cat to dislike a smell that protects us." But her smile soon faded because she did not feel the little pouch beneath her own undershirt. Her heart skipped a beat, and she was afraid that she'd lost the little bag. Now she felt very guilty that she'd taken it off before entering school. Quickly, she searched her book bag and sighed with great relief when she found the aromatic pouch. She felt that luck touched her twice that day; first because Mama forgot to check for the Asefetida bags when the girls got home from school, which she usually did, and second because she found the bag and had it safely on again.

Mama was uncompromising about the twins wearing their Asefetida bags. Most children in the neighborhood wore one as a health precaution. The contents of the bag were reputed to ward off diseases, like tuberculosis and scarlet fever, which were then rampant in urban areas. Mama prepared the bags herself and sewed a small pouch from white muslin. She bought the Asefetida, a yellow-brown herbal mixture, and a block

14

of camphor at the drug store. She crushed the ingredients together and filled the small pouches. Finally, she stitched them closed. The girls' body heat caused the camphor to melt, and the smells mingled. Sometimes the bags stained their undershirts with dark spots. But, Mama believed in the mixture's protection, and carefully laundered the shirts to get out the stains. The girls knew that if their Mama told them to wear the bags, it was very important to wear the bags. They never challenged Mama in such matters. Yet, the smell that the pouch emitted was very annoying, so they cheated...a little...feeling guilty all the while. (They never did get scarlet fever or tuberculosis, but they did have the mumps, the measles and the chicken pox.)

The immediate neighborhood of Gates Avenue was like a pocket in which people of different backgrounds lived harmoniously. The neighborhood melded successfully because most of the people were poor, hardworking, proud of where they lived and proud of their accomplishments that could not be measured by money. And they cared for one another. Mothers looked out for each other's children, and the children played together. In this tiny geographic pocket, the rich ethnic mix worked like an extended family, and the DeSaussures were part of the blend. They felt no hatred and heard no racial slurs. This was a neighborhood that nurtured respect. It was home.

The Pigis, an Italian-American family, lived next door. The adults and children were good friends. The families exchanged gifts at Christmas and wished each

15

other well. Mrs. Pigi brought over lasagna, and Mr. Pigi gave Daddy a bottle of his homemade wine, made from the grapes that he grew in his backyard. Mama gave the Pigi's a freshly baked cake. In good weather, the Pigis invited the men of the neighborhood to play bocci on their court. Daddy explained to the girls that the game originated in Italy and was played almost always only by men.

Grandma Pigi sat on an empty wooden milk crate in front of the Pigi house, when the weather was warm enough for her. She wore dark clothes and seemed always to be busy knitting. Her needles moved quickly, even though her fingers were swollen from arthritis. Willie would watch the ball of yarn at Grandma's feet become smaller and smaller, while what she was knitting became larger and larger. Grandma often smiled at Willie. One day, Grandma was so engrossed in her work and thoughts that she did not see Willie approach her until she felt a gentle tap on her shoulder. She nodded to acknowledge Willie's presence. Then, speaking with a heavy Italian accent she said, "Buena sierre, Willie, whatta you uppa to today? You know how to knit?"

"No, Miss Pigi, but I'd like to learn."

"Then, sitta down child, and watch me maka the stitches. Ask you mother to getta you some wool, and I teach you to maka sweater and scarf."

Willie watched the needles and wool for a while as Grandma Pigi worked them very slowly. She got the

16

hang of how the wool was worked around the needles and then smiled up at Grandma. "I better go home now; Mama will be looking for me." Grandma Pigi smiled back. Willie was thrilled that she would be knitting and thought, *Soon I'll be able to make the best sweater in the world!*

The next day, Willie returned with two balls of wool. Grandma Pigi entrusted her with a pair of knitting needles and began her lessons. Willie was good, and her fingers soon moved fast and precisely. Within a few weeks she finished a sweater. She was the envy of the twins, who then also wanted Grandma Pigi to teach them to knit, too.

The twins shared a love of candy, and the little candy store down the block was a magnet for neighborhood children. A Jewish couple from Eastern Europe owned it. They spoke with a heavy Yiddish accent, but that didn't stop the children from understanding them. The smell of homemade sweets presented a warm welcome to everyone. The chubby owners looked like they must have tasted and liked much of their own candy. The multicolored sweets were displayed in large and small glass jars and in a glass counter. Mary and Martha were delighted by the happy colors and sweet aroma. Their dark eyes took in all the items. They checked their purses and jiggled their coins more than once.

"Vell children, vhat vilst du?" asked the heavy woman.

17

Without hesitating or consulting with her sister, Mary answered, "The Penny Prize Bag, please."

This marvelous bag of sweets was usually enough for three children, but now the lucky girls would have to share it only with each other. To their added joy, they still had a few dimes left over after they paid for the candy. They had saved their presents from their aunts' and uncles' last visits. Mama and Daddy were in no financial position to give the twins money to spend on candy. They were working hard just to provide the children's necessities. So this candy was an extra special bonus.

The girls didn't get as far as the door of the shop before they opened the bag. They looked inside at the sweets, then at each other. Their eyes were shining, their smiles were wide, and they could not wait one minute longer to actually taste their candy. Each girl very delicately chose a piece, then with very ladylike manners slowly placed it into her mouth. With their eyes closed, they allowed the first pieces of sweetness to melt slowly in their mouths to get their full taste. Then they licked their sticky fingers, not wanting to waste even the slightest trace of taste. But, somehow, before they left the store, the bag became half empty! Martha had a small pang of guilt and said, "We should give Willie a taste." She forced herself to look serious. But, when she looked at the expression on Mary's face, she burst out laughing. Whereupon each girl grabbed another piece of candy...and then another.

Very soon, Mary looked into the bag and with a playful frown murmured, "Too late, Willie; better luck next time." (The candy store was later sold to the Knights, a West-Indian family, who kept up the tradition of handmade delicacies.)

The Kosher delicatessen down the street was another favorite. Willie, Martha and Mary loved their long kosher hot dogs smothered with mustard on a bed of sauerkraut surrounded by a huge, soft bun. The perfectly cooked frankfurter made a distinct crunching sound when it was bitten into, and the girls had to be very careful to keep the hot, spicy juice that burst out of its skin in their mouths, not dribbling down their chins onto their clothing. Mama would be very angry if, in addition to her own work, she had to worry about getting stubborn stains out of the girls' clothes. As an extra treat, the warm-hearted store owners often gave the girls a free sour pickle. And when the girls occasionally didn't have enough money for two franks, they got two anyway, and were trusted to bring in the money another day.

The neighborhood also had a beauty parlor owned by an Italian-American family, the Spear's corner grocery, Giordano's Fish Market, Harry's Butcher Shop, Cohen's Drug Store and Ice Cream Parlor, and Mrs. Hardy's and Mrs. Reilly's Thrift Shop that dealt in new and used clothing.

Everyone loved Mrs. Spear and called her "Mama." She was a hard working, Jewish woman, who allowed her customers to "buy on the book"—pay their bills as money became available.

Mama DeSaussure bought her Sunday dinner chicken, usually a hen that weighed about four pounds, from Harry. He always had a kindly manner towards her. "How's the minister and the girls? I have a beautiful bird for your dinner, weighs just over four pounds." He would wink his left eye as he put the chicken on the scale. "Yep, it sure weighs over four pounds, I'll only charge you for four—enjoy."

Mama'd answer, with a big smile, "God bless you, Mr. Harry."

The Cohens served the most delicious egg-creams, ice cream sodas and banana splits. Their portions went to the top of the glasses.

Mama's favorite place was the Thrift Shop, owned by two elegant, sophisticated Black ladies. They were both top-notch seamstresses, who made clothes to-order for their richer clients. They were proud of their relationship with the world-renowned singer, Billie Holiday, and a collection of her autographed photographs decorated a wall of their shop. Their specialty item was expensive handmade Corday bags, which were sold to rich society ladies. They often helped out when eighth-grade schoolgirls were late with or unable to hand-sew their own graduation dresses. Although Mrs. Reilly and Mrs. Hardy came to their immediate rescue, the girls had to forfeit high grades in sewing class later.

20

Mama saw the thrift shop as a wonderland of bargains. Mrs. Hardy made sure to save the least worn clothes for Mama and her girls, and would welcome Mama each time she came. "I've some fine things for you from a recent shipment, Mrs. DeSaussure. This will fit Willie. This has only a small stain. This one has a tiny hole in the collar." Mama'd look each item over carefully, saying, "I can easily fix that," or "I can take care of that."

Mrs. Hardy was obviously happy to work with Mama, because Mama had a good eye—the ability to see value beyond a little surface blemish—and good hands—the ability to fix an imperfection. "Mrs. DeSaussure, you sure do know how to make your young ones look good."

Although the twins had a good feeling about belonging in the "pocket neighborhood," outside of the safe-zone they bore Mama'a words of caution, "Be very careful where you are not always welcome." Willie, Martha, and Mary knew that Stuyvesant Heights had mean streets with its problems right out in the open. Fistfights, knifings, store break-ins, gang rumbles and "turf" wars did happen. Yet, that reality had little to do with them, because they were occupied with church, school and family life. That violence was removed, something to be aware of, but not personal to them.

But on a very personal level, they were hurt when nasty stares, superior airs and racial slurs were thrown at them. The checker in a Food Fair Supermarket, who yelled at them, "Get out! We don't want niggers here!";

21

the little white girl in Victory Field Park in Queens who pointed and yelled to her mother as Mary ran by, "Look Mama! Look at that chocolate girl!"; the Black school kids, who were lighter skinned, who acted superior and wouldn't invite them to their parties. That all hurt.

Mary wrestled with her thoughts about being dark skinned, and one day asked Mama why she'd married such a dark-skinned man. "If Daddy had been lighter, so would we. Wouldn't we?" Mary asked. She thought long about what her life would be like if she were white, or very light skinned, until Daddy's words became clear in her mind.

"You must never challenge God's plan for each of us. You must trust in Him completely." And so she did, and let her fantasy go. From that time on, Mary was to find pride in herself, her accomplishments and her rich color.

CHAPTER 3

"Hey, get up, get up, we've got lots to do, its Saturday!" Willie said in a soft voice while giving each of the twins' feet a playful kick.

"I wanna go back to sleep," each one whined. "It's too early." They looked at Willie through sleep-heavy eyes.

"Mama will have a fit if we don't get up and help Daddy with the cleaning," Willie continued, "You know Daddy's the handyman for this whole house, and he can't do everything. The cleaning's our job."

After complaining a little more and yawning as they dressed, the girls were ready for Saturday morning prayer and breakfast. Then Mama assigned each of them a household task.

The twins liked to work together. They took turns with Willie working inside and outside the apartment. Willie readily accepted Mama's assignments. Sometimes the twins rebelled, but Willie, in her quiet way, ignored their rebellion, motivated them, and the work got done. Hallways of the three-story building had to be swept from top to bottom. Daddy made sure the stairwells were spotless and the wooden banisters polished. Even the steps outside the house had to be swept and washed. In their own apartment, the kitchen floor had to be washed and waxed, and all the surfaces had to be dusted.

23

Then, Saturday afternoon was free time. Willie tended to her dolls' clothing, washing, starching and ironing it. And she sewed, crocheted, or knit. She inherited Mama's golden fingers. The twins often delivered clothing for Mr. Griffin, a friendly but stern black gentleman, who owned the neighborhood Tailoring and Dry Cleaning store.

They had approached him one day after brainstorming how to make money to go to the movies. They asked him, "Mr. Griffin, do you need anyone to carry clothes to your customers? We want to earn money to go to the movies. Our parents can't afford to give us any extra money."

Mr. Griffin seemed to appreciate their honesty and thought a moment as he looked into each girl's face. "Wait a minute," he said, "I think I have some tailoring over here waiting to be delivered." He smiled as he looked through his racks of clothing. "These folks wanted their delivery before Sunday...and so did these. If you work for me, you'll have to be extra careful not to drop anything."

The girls were ecstatic. They had a real job. They could earn spending money! They made twenty-five cents for each delivery, and sometimes as much as a dime tip. They never used public transportation, and ran to make all the deliveries.

Then, still bursting with youthful excitement after getting their last delivery done, they would run to the Sumner Theater to meet their friends, and to thrill to a western or a musical on the big screen. Fred Astaire, Ginger Rogers, and Gene Kelly were their favorite actors.

Willie, Mary, and Martha had a special quick task on Saturday. Mr. Rachel, or the rabbi from the synagogue, needed their help, because orthodox Jewish people did not work on the Sabbath, the day of rest. Turning lights on and off in the synagogue was considered work. Each of the girls had a turn at putting the lights on in the synagogue and turning them off. This was done at a designated time. They helped out during other Jewish holidays, too. Daddy insisted that the girls accept no money for this task and told them sternly, "You are not to take money for helping the Jewish people obey their Lord. Just follow Mr. Rachel's or the rabbi's directions." The girls felt a particular joy to be so needed and to be in such a position to help.

Daddy was proud of his girls doing the Lord's work. He would say, "These poor people would have to pray in the dark, if you didn't help out." Daddy tried always to instill in his children the love of all people. "Forget about color. Beneath this skin we are all the same. God loves everyone, and we have to respect all people," he preached. He taught his children about the special connection between Black people and Hebrew people, who many years ago also had been slaves. And he reminded the girls to watch their manners, "Be on time, be respectful in any house of God, don't act up or do foolish things in the synagogue."

25

The girls found the synagogue a very strange church. There were no crosses, no pictures of Jesus, and no statues of the holy family. It was dim inside this sanctuary. Men and women did not sit together as in Daddy's church. The women and girls sat in the balcony section. The men and boys sat in the main area, near the altar. The sisters often arrived early, before the services were over, hoping to hear the cantor's beautiful singing voice. Some of the melodies reminded them of the hymns they sang at Sunday worship. Daddy told them that many of their own gospel songs were influenced by the text of the Old Testament, and the lamenting sounds of the Hebrew prayers.

They were still in awe of the prayer ceremony weeks later as they watched and listened to men draped in prayer shawls, totally engrossed in their worship, slowly sway as they prayed. The first time they beheld this ritual and seemed perplexed, Mr. Rachel carefully explained to them the customs and religious objects used in the synagogue.

Now, they looked forward each week to the religious singing and ceremony and to being part of something important.

26

CHAPTER 4

The cold February temperatures and ongoing grayness of the snow-filled skies combined to make life somewhat boring. The drabness of the days and the dirty snow that slowly melted in the streets had everyone feeling tired and irritable. But today, Saturday, was an oddity. It was a warmer day, the morning sky was overcast as usual, but the air began to move. Dark, heavy clouds rolled over Stuyvesant Heights and threatened to spill their load. Anticipation of a change filled the air.

Mama summoned Mary and Martha to go to the grocery store to buy a loaf of bread and a five-gallon can of kerosene oil. The twins, charged with energy, were eager to go outside, do their chore, meet their friends, and run. Mama instructed the girls to return immediately after shopping, before the wet snow came and the streets were filled with slush. Mary carried the empty can. Both girls smiled broadly. Mama carefully braided their hair and decorated it with colorful clips. They looked neat and happy—but their shining dark eyes almost gave away the mischief they were planing.

The girls ran to the grocery store on Sumner Avenue, a straight block and a half from their home. They took a round-about route that day and laughed all the way. Approaching the store from the far side, they were surprised to see a stream of children leaving buses and cars that snaked their way along the road to the 13th

27

Regiment Armory, which was about four blocks away from the grocery store. The twins looked at each other in wonder, and then became curious enough to investigate.

"Martha, lets go see what they are doing."

"I don't know...maybe we should just get the oil and bread and just go home."

"Come on Martha, please. Let's take a chance. Let's run up to the Armory just to see what's up. Please!"

The girls sped to the Armory, but the big door was shut. Mary reached up to the high handle to open it just a bit. At that instant, the door opened and the girls looked up at a tall, white man looking down at them. "Yes?" He said.

Mary found her voice and asked, "We saw a lot of children going in here. What's going on?"

"It's a track meet, little girl. Come on in."

As the twins entered the cavernous, brightly-lit hall which was filled wall-to-wall with children and noise, the door slammed shut behind them.

"Would you like to run?" the man asked.

Martha and Mary looked at each other in amazement, each twin hoping to find approval in the face of the other. Mary spoke first, sensing the urgency of giving an answer. "Yes, can I? Please let me run."

The man looked at Mary and frowned at her. "You can't run like that," he said quietly.

Mary looked at her long, green and beige woolen dress. *It does have a tiny moth hole, or two,* she thought. *The dress is okay.* Then she looked at her feet, at the black galoshes that covered the green shoes with the small Cuban heels that she had secretly borrowed from Willie. *Well, the streets are wet,* she thought, as she met the man's gaze.

The man smiled, and said again, "You can't run like that."

"Yes I can. Please let me."

Another official came over an said, "We gotta get underway. Little girl, if you put on your gym suit and sneakers you may run."

The other children were getting quiet, waiting for the race to begin.

Mary's lip trembled. She held back tears. Her eyes met the man's. "I don't own any gym suit or sneakers. Please, please let me run...I can even run against the wind."

The officials looked at each other, shocked by the spunky little girl. "Let's let her run," they said. Then they turned to Martha. "Do you want to run, too?"

Too shocked and amazed at what was happening to Mary, Martha was speechless, then managed to say, "No thank you," just as Mary handed her her coat.

The other official swooped Mary up and stood her on a scale in the corner. The officials looked at the scale then at each other. "She is a fine weight for the 40-yard dash."

Mary and Martha looked at each other and then around them. The hall seemed to swallow them up. Theirs were the only black faces in sight. The twins stepped closer together and stood still, unlike the other children who jumped up and down with excitement. The twins' eyes shown with anticipation.

Mary was first to take her place on the line in the first heat. She waited quietly. The other five girls were excited and moved around restlessly. The official approached Mary and said, "Little girl, I'm going to tell you what this race is about. There are several races that we call heats. Try to win your heat. The winner of each heat will move up. You could move up into the finals." He stopped talking for a second and pointed out the path of her heat. "This is your course. I am going to say to all of you running 'get on your mark... get set...go!'" He pointed to the floor. "This is your starting mark. Little girl, when I say 'go,' you fly!"

Martha stood near by listening to the official. She thought to herself, *I can't believe it. Mary's really going to run!*

Mary's heart was pounding in her ears. The hall became a blur, and she did not look at the other children in her race. She focused on the finish line, determined to run as she had never run before. She barley heard the command, "GO!" A few seconds later she felt a

30

burning on her neck. It was the sisal rope at the finish line. Mary had won her first race!

The official asked her to wait at the line, and Martha approached her. Suddenly, Mary's twinkling eyes dropped to the empty kerosene can that Martha was holding. The sisters' eyes locked for an instant.

"Martha," Mary whispered, "we're gonna get it. We were supposed to go to the store for bread and kerosene. What are we going to do?"

Martha raised her eyebrows and replied matter-of-factly, "I'm going to the balcony to get a better view of what's going on. Period. We are here now...and you won your race!"

The balcony was packed, and Martha was excited. She listened to the grown-ups talking about Betty Hermann, a popular runner from the German-American Track Club. She was considered a favorite, a star, and Martha knew Mary would be running against her. When she thought of the consequences for not coming home on time, she was frightened. Daddy's braided clothesline would surely appear for both of them, even if Mary won. She thought, *Our coming home late is a sure act of disobedience, and Daddy will get us just like he does when we get poor grades in school.* Her heart beat wildly. She pushed to the front of the balcony to look over the railing. Just as she got to the railing there was a lot of screaming and laughing. Wearing her green and beige woolen dress, and green Cuban-heeled shoes, Mary had won her second race, and now stood alone

31

at the finish line. The other runners wore blue or green gym suits and white sneakers. *Mary sure sticks out,* Martha thought. And people were asking, "Who is that little Black girl? Where did she come from? Who does she run for?"

Martha didn't say a word. Although she was bursting with excitement over her sister's achievement, she managed to keep quiet, not to call attention to herself, and to watch as Mary continued to win heats and move into the finals.

Finally, there was Betty Hermann with her pigtails, flying as she ran her hardest. And there was Mary, blazing ahead of her to the sisal rope. *Mary won!* But when the girls lined up for their awards, Mary's bright smile turned into a puzzled expression. Although she was happy to have the medal in her hands, she looked at the official with a question in her eyes. The medal was *silver*, not the gold one for First Place.

Seeing her disappointment the official said quietly to her, "Don't worry. You'll be one of the three girl finalists, and you will have a chance for a gold medal at Madison Square Garden. Run like today, and you'll be a champ!"

Martha skipped down the balcony stairs and ran to Mary and said, "Girl, come on! Let's go now! Daddy will beat us for sure."

As the girls turned toward the door, a uniformed Parks Department official approached them. Mary had easily seen the Black man in the crowd earlier and wondered who he was. His uniform was as neat as a pin. He carried his winter coat folded over his arm. The girls were happy to see another Black person. He spoke to them. "I'm William Jackson from the Sumner Avenue Playground. I'm on my lunch break, and I have seen some of the races. Frankly, I am amazed at your spunkiness, young lady." He looked at Mary, then shifted his gaze to Martha, "Little girl, you with her?"

Martha answered, speaking more quickly than the man was expecting. "Yes, but you know what? Our father is going to reprimand us...we are going to get a beating when we get home...we have been out for four or five hours...we are really afraid to go home."

Mr. Jackson looked into Martha's eyes and then into Mary's. "I do understand the seriousness of your situation," he said, "I'll go home with you two and help explain what has happened here."

But Martha was so excited and worried, she did not hear his offer and after a quivering deep breath continued with her own thoughts, "Oh, please, would you come with us? You could explain to our father that Mary won...that they want her to go to Madison Square Garden to run...she's gotta have sneakers...she's gotta have a gym suit or shorts...'n' everything to go..."

Mr. Jackson cut into Martha's rushing words, "I'll go with you. I'm nearby at the park." Now that he had Martha's attention he meant to hold it and said, "You're twins, and with your sister running like that, I'll bet you can run too. Am I right?"

This time Martha was right on target with her answer. "I jump a lot of Double Dutch, and I run all the time. I'm about as fast as Mary."

"I'm very impressed," said Mr. Jackson. "You girls should get two or three more girls to join you and start a team like the German-Americans girls did."

CHAPTER 5

It was dark outside and sleeting when Willie looked through the bedroom window. She was worried about the twins. As a roll of thunder rumbled over head, Willie put her fingertips against the glass and felt it shake. Crashing thunder made her shake, too.

What freak weather, she thought. *Where are those twins? I sure hope they are somewhere inside. I bet they are at the candy store listening to the jukebox and dancing. But, this time, things feel different. They've never been out in the dark before without permission, and Daddy is furious.*

Daddy was pacing up and down the living room with his whipping strap in his hand. "When they get home, they're gonna get it. Mama it's about time one of us went out and started looking for them."

Knowing how mischievous the twins could be, Mama tried to calm Daddy, and at least keep him home. The twins could be in an undesirable place, and Daddy would be sure to find them. "Oh, B, you know how the girls are. Don't be too angry, I'm sure they are not in any danger and probably waiting out the storm with their friends," she said, all the while trying to hide her own fear.

"Boy, are we in trouble, trouble, trouble," Martha and Mary said in unison. They quickly looked at each

35

other and rushed out of the Armory. Mary held the silver medal tightly in her left hand and clutched the big envelope with the important papers in her right. The twins were very nervous even though Mr. Jackson was going home with them. Their hearts pounded as they ran through the wet streets. The empty kerosene can made a hollow sound as it banged against Mary's legs. Finally, they reached the door of the apartment and discovered that not only had they no bread and no kerosene, they'd also left their key inside the apartment. They had to ring the bell, and face their parents right at the door!

Mama opened the door. At first her eyes were wide with surprise. She sighed deeply, grateful to see her missing little girls. "Thank God you are here," she said. Then her anger and the volume of her voice began to rise. "Come right in! Where were you?!" Mama rarely raised her voice; the girls knew she was very, very angry.

Mary quickly whispered, "We were at the track meet."

Mama, glancing at Mr. Jackson said, "Who sent you there? And who is this man?"

Mary answered, "Oh, Mama, don't beat me. I won. See my medal! I can run in Madison Square Garden, where Joe Louis boxes. Mr. Jackson will explain everything." Mary's eyes implored Mr. Jackson to do a good job.

Mama settled her gaze on Mr. Jackson and crossed her arms, waiting to hear his story.

His tone was gentlemanly as he began to speak, first introducing himself and then relating the day's events. He explained that a city-wide "Olympic Sports Carnival" was planned for Madison Square Garden and that preliminary track meets were going on in every borough. Finalists represented parks and playgrounds of each area. His own playground on Sumner Avenue, which was formerly an old horse barn owned by the Sheffield Milk Company, had been finished only a few weeks before the Brooklyn competitions and was too new to send representatives to the Preliminaries at the 13th Regiment Armory. Mary had won the competition and had received a silver medal. Unfortunately, she had no way to protest a silver medal that should have been the gold because she was not officially representing a park or playground. In answer to Mama's raised eyebrows he said, "Yes, she really did place first. I know she feels she was cheated out of the gold medal because she is a Negro. He paused for a moment and then ended by saying, "I came home with your children because they knew that they were out too late, and that probably you and their father were waiting to punish them when they got home. I am here to save them from that. Your daughter really ran a fantastic race at the Armory, and she really does have a chance to go to Madison Square Garden in the spring. I would like to explain to you what should be done now, if you want her to take advantage of this opportunity."

Daddy slowly came into the dinning room, where the little group had moved to. He had been absorbed in reading the Bible and preparing his sermon when the bell rang. When he looked at the girls and the strange man in his home, he appeared to be getting even more excited than Mama was. Mary took a step toward him, and he used his most forceful voice to say, "Sit down!"

She sat.

Daddy sat. He slowly pulled the braided clothesline across his lap.

Mr. Jackson introduced himself to Daddy and repeated what he had told Mama.

Daddy looked at Martha sitting across from him. Then he looked into Mary's eyes. He spoke in a measured, angry-sounding tone to both of them. "What time did you leave this morning?"

Mary's quivery, hushed voice answered, "At 10:30 Daddy."

"What were you told to do?"

Mary again answered. "Get a loaf of bread and a can of kerosene oil."

"Well, what happened?"

Mary began speaking very rapidly, and because she was nervous left out some details. "Daddy, I saw a lot of children going into the Armory...and I was curious... and I realized I could run, too...and I wanted to run." She looked into his eyes, and she spoke, "Look," her

38

little hands brought Daddy the envelope of papers, "Read all my paperwork before you beat me."

Daddy gave Mama a puzzled look. Mama said, "I don't really know what it's about, B." Daddy read the papers.

Mary was very excited, but she spoke softly. "Daddy," she said, "I can do it, I can run. See my silver medal."

Daddy looked at the medal and then back at Mama. Then speaking in his Sunday Church Service voice he said, "You were disobedient, but I'm going to forgive you." His gaze shifted to Mama. "Mama, go to the store on Monday, and buy Mary a gym suit and sneakers."

Mama knew that this expense would be a burden on the family's small income, but she and Daddy kept this adult problem to themselves. She looked at Mr. Jackson, who nodded and smiled knowingly at her.

Mary clapped her hands and jumped around joyously, hugging everyone in the room including Flossie.

"Now, I have to leave and close the park," said Mr. Jackson as he rose and shook hands with Daddy. "Good-bye to you all for a while, and congratulations!"

Willie sat quietly listening to the goings-on. She was surprised that the twins were not given beatings.

Mary looked at Martha intently and thought, *This must be one of those miracles Daddy always speaks of....*

CHAPTER 6

It was supper time. Daddy summoned the whole family to the dining room, where he took his seat at the head of the set table. He was ready to say grace. He asked each member of the family to recite a Bible verse from memory. Mary always tried to be first in order to have a chance at the shortest verse. She blurted out, "Jesus wept." Daddy was surprised by her quick answer and seemed a little disappointed. He looked into Mary's eyes and said in his commanding voice, "Mary, you should be more grateful, you had quite a day. Don't always look for the shortest way out. Tonight would have been a good time to say a longer verse, and thank God for your good luck."

Daddy is just preaching again, Mary thought, *but maybe I'd better say a longer verse tomorrow. I don't want God to be mad at me. I don't want to lose the race at Madison Square Garden.*

After each member of the family recited a verse, Daddy proclaimed, "Let's eat!" and Mama brought in the supper: fried porgies, collard greens, sweet potatoes, and a big bowl of rice. This was the family's favorite meal and brought memories of South Carolina to Mama and Daddy. Dessert was special, too. It was made of layers of graham crackers spread with chocolate pudding. It had been chilled in the icebox. This was an economical wartime sweet treat that became a family favorite, and all eyes watched as Mama cut equal, generous portions for everyone. When the last crumb disappeared into Martha's mouth from her fingertip, Mama and Daddy exchanged smiles. Mama then announced, "Time to do the dishes."

The smiling girls suddenly stared at each other. This was a chore they didn't like to do, but they dutifully followed Mama into the kitchen. Mama carefully washed each dish in a large, deep pan filled with sudsy water. Then she dipped the dish in a pan of clear water to remove the soap. Martha dried, and Willie put the dishes away in the high cabinets.

Preparations for Sunday began right after the last dish was put away. Shoes were polished, special dresses and clean socks were laid out, and Saturday night baths were taken. Bathing took time, because large pots of water had to be heated, carried to the bathroom, and poured into the deep claw-footed tub. The family lived in a cold water flat. Mama carried the heavy pots of steaming, sloshing water and moved very careful, hoping not to burn herself. Each girl got clean water. Mary was first into the tub while Martha and Willie mumbled their resignation. "Yeah, let her have her way tonight. Miss Big Shot Runner." Daddy and Mama took their turns after the children.

Daddy prepared his Sunday sermon on Saturday evening. Except for the purring of Flossie at Daddy's feet and the occasional rustle of note paper or a page of the Bible, the room was quiet. With his sermon completed, Daddy tuned in country-western music on the radio. Sometimes he would relax by crocheting. He

41

taught himself from a book and now his home was filled with his beautiful antimacassars that decorated the furniture. Willie often watched him crochet in silence, learning the skill herself. Once he surprised her with a crocheted blouse. Daddy was also a talented poet and wrote the Christmas ballad, "The Little Boy."

By nine o'clock, bedtime, the girls were ready to go off to their room and their queen-sized bed. Martha and Mary slept side by side, and because they were little, there was room for Willie across the bottom. The twins were still excited and chattered about the happenings of the day. Mary put her silver medal under her pillow, Willie listened to her sisters patiently, but felt a little envy in her heart because she had not been part of the monumental event. Even with the light off the twins giggled and squirmed around in their bed until late into the night, shushing each other constantly. They were so excited, they even forgot to say their prayers. Finally, exhaustion overcame them, and the curtain of silence dropped on Saturday.

The Little Boy

Rev. W.D. DeSaussure

This little boy gave them to remember,
That He was born the 25th of December;
Lawyers and doctors they got amazed,
But they had to give that little boy praise.

Chorus:

Now little boy how old are you,
Now little boy how old are you,
Now little boy how old are you,
Sir, I am only twelve years old.

Lawyers and doctors stood and wondered,
As though they had been struck by thunder,
Then they decided while they wondered,
That all mankind must come under.

This little boy grew and got strong;
His mother and father kept leading Him on,
And on their return from Jerusalem,
They looked for the boy but He was gone.

This little boy He had the key,
To unfold hidden mysteries;
Then they decided wise as He,
We'd better let that little boy be.

43

Lawyers and doctors put Him to test,
Asking Him about that heavenly rest;
But He explained to their consternation,
That He came to die for their salvation.

John carried Him in Jordan's deep,
The Holy Ghost from heaven did leap;
And when the water parted over,
The Holy Ghost leaped upon His shoulder.

The last time the little boy was seen,
He was standing on Mt. Olivet's green.
And after dispersing of the crowd,
He entered up into a cloud.

The little boy was Jesus Christ,
He died to give the world eternal life;
All in Him who do believe,
The blessed Holy Ghost you'll receive.

As He ascended to the heavenly land,
He was seen by the waving of His hand;
Teach all nations My command,
And lo, I am with you till the world shall end.

CHAPTER 7

Sunlight streamed into the girls' room. They had forgotten to pull the shades down the night before. Even Mama, who always seemed to think of everything, forgot to remind them. Mama's voice sounded reveille like a bugle, "Hey! Wake up! Mary! Martha! Willie!"

Willie awakened first and touched Mary and Martha's feet lightly. She got no response, so she gave them each a kick. The night was too short for the youngsters who had fooled around and talked too long. Willie delivered another kick, harder. Finally two sets of dark eyes opened reluctantly and proved the girls were awake. The aroma of frying bacon drifting in from the kitchen pulled the girls out of bed. Then they stampeded toward the bathroom to wash. Willie was the first into the bathroom because she was the first one up. She flashed her sisters a wide, victory grin. Dutifully, Mary and Martha had to wait.

Mama had been up since five o'clock preparing the family's special Sunday morning breakfast—scrambled eggs, grits, yeast rolls and bacon. The girls hurried to sit down at the set table as Mama filled their cups with freshly brewed tea or Postum, a coffee substitute. The family did not drink real coffee. Daddy was the last one to arrive at the table, because he was the last one to use the bathroom. Today was a day that he did not

45

have to rush. Church did not begin until eleven o'clock. This schedule suited everyone.

The girls prepared for Sunday School. They would feel beautiful in their "Sunday dresses," navy blue wool dresses with little lace collars, and their cranberry red coats and matching hats with the "fur" trim. Mama carefully braided their hair and adorned the braids with blue ribbons and barrettes that matched their dresses. Willie styled her own hair into a pompadour and debated between adding an artificial rose or her favorite flowery headband.

Daddy was very much the picture of a minister in his black, pin-stripe suit, dark gray Stetson hat with the little golden feather in its black band, and black wing-tip shoes. He carried his long, black wool winter coat over his arm. Mama was lovely in her shiny black seal coat and black shoes and matching purse. She loved the soft, smooth feel of the coat.

It was important to Daddy that the family dress appropriately for Sunday worship. He had a charge account at Uneedas, a small department store in Jamaica, Queens. From time to time the family would go there by elevated train to buy coats and dresses. The charge account allowed Daddy to pay his bills in small installments.

At nine, the girls rushed across the street to the store-front church for Sunday School. Only a few children attended, and they all contributed their thoughts about the Bible story that was being studied. School

46

took an hour and a half. Later, the children would join their parents for family worship in the same little room.

Daddy's church services were lively, and long. The room shook with the rhythm of gospel singing and hand clapping. High-spirited worshipers heartily joined Daddy in the service, and Mama's clear soprano voice soared above the others. Mary led the singing of the hymn, "Pass Me Not, Oh Gentle Savior." But the focus of the service was always Daddy's sermon.

After the service, Daddy stood at the door of the room and had short talks with his parishioners. When the last one left, he closed the door and guided his family home, across the street. Mama walked with pride beside her husband, and the children felt truly happy to be the minister's children.

Once home, the girls quickly changed out of their "Sunday dresses" and into everyday clothes. They would play in their room the rest of the day while ministers from other Brooklyn parishes visited Daddy and had lively discussions about the Bible and the sermons each one gave. Mama made sure the guests were accorded respect, and monitored the noise from the girls' room carefully. A tap on their door was usually enough to quiet them down. So, while the men talked, she bustled about the kitchen, completing a special Sunday dinner.

Two huge pots were on the stove top. One contained fluffy white rice, the other had chicken feet, back and neck pieces, salt pork, onions, celery, pieces of bell pepper, flour, water and spices simmering in it. Dinner would be chicken stew and rice, fried chicken pieces, potato salad, collard greens and homemade ice cream.

Daddy would eat with his company. Mama and the girls ate after the gentlemen left. Sometimes, Mama was annoyed that the men helped themselves to more than one portion of chicken and left little for the girls. But there was usually enough of the other foods to feed them amply. When there were no guests, the family ate together.

Sometimes, when the weather was warmer, in the spring and summer, gospel singers would stroll through the neighborhood at suppertime, singing and stopping at windows until people threw some change into their tambourines. The girls did not want to part with their candy money, but Mamma was soft-hearted. "Even if we are poor, they may be worse off than we are. You have to know the meaning of giving, sharing, not being selfish." Reluctantly, the girls threw down some of their pennies.

When Reverend DeSaussure had no company for dinner, the family walked to the Fulton Street Park. This was a treat for the girls, who were allowed to climb and hang on the monkey bars and run around. They could sing out and really cut up. Often, during these evenings, it seemed as though the whole neighborhood was out for an early evening stroll. Families would meet and exchange pleasantries. The men would tip their hats in respect to the ladies of the house, and parents engaged in small talk about their children.

Returning home after sundown, the girls walked in front of their watchful parents.

Once in a while a few of Daddy's friends would stay into the evening, and the whole family would be asked to join them in the living room. The girls played the piano. Willie was certainly the best, but Mary and Martha would have made their piano teacher, Mrs. Ambrister, smile too.

Mrs. Ambrister was a gentle Black lady from Bermuda, and a strict teacher. "Practice, practice, practice, and you could end up in Carnegie Hall," she would say. "I will make you into a Beethoven or a Chopin!" Her tapping foot was her students' metronome. Most neighborhood children took piano lessons from Mrs. Ambrister.

Usually, Sunday night was radio night. The family sat facing the tall, brown Emerson cabinet that stood on the living room floor. Lamont Cranston was "The Shadow" and Daddy was his accomplice in mystery as he turned off all the lights to heighten the feeling of scariness. The girls screamed with fear at the show's realistic sound effects, but loved every minute of it.

Two broadcasts for the night were the limit Daddy set. The girls would often chose a western, "Baby Snooks," or "Blondie." After the second show, Daddy would say, "You've had two, now it's time for bed."

Daddy, Mama, Willie after Sunday service, 1943.

Mama after
Sunday service,
1945.

50

Daddy with a friend, 1945.

CHAPTER 8

As promised, Mama bought Mary a gym suit and white sneakers a few days later. It was a light green bloomer-style suit. In the evening, Mary modeled it for the family and twirled around the room saying, "Daddy, I'll be the best runner in the whole city; just you watch me!"

Daddy knew that his little girl had the spunk of a giant. Now he was amused by her attitude and said in a soft, yet determined tone, "Mary, now don't you look fine. Be sure you always act nice, do your best. Make us proud."

As Mary looked at herself in the mirror, she thought how the mint green gym suit contrasted with her dark brown skin, and she began to think about her silver medal. *Maybe if I wasn't Black, I wouldn't have been cheated out of the gold medal....* But Martha and Willie, fingering the texture of the gym suit's material, broke into her thoughts. Their eyes were wide with wonder and they began pulling on the fabric. "Get off me!" Mary yelled. "Mama, they're teasing me!"

Mama came to Mary's rescue and said sternly, "Leave her be. This suit must stay clean and last. We don't have any money to buy her another one!"

The following day, Mary and Martha were sent on a shopping errand. Again, they chose to run to the grocery store on Sumner Avenue, but they warned each

52

other, "No stopping. We gotta get home as soon as possible." As they were leaving the store with their purchases, Mary saw a man waving to them and calling them from across the street. It was Mr. Jackson. He walked over to them and said, "I just wanted to wish you good luck." He smiled and gave Mary the "V" for victory sign. "Let me know how you do at The Garden." Then he turned and walked back to his Sumner Street Playground. The twins looked at each other and shared the thought, *He's gonna be a friend.*

Since the Preliminaries at the Armory, February and a good part of March had passed. It was time for Mary to run in Madison Square Garden, and Mama took the girls into Manhattan. There were only a few black participants, and Mary had no trouble spotting Mama, Willie, and Martha in the audience even though they seemed to be swallowed up in the huge crowd. She just looked for the dark dots in the sea of white faces. As she looked around the large hall she thought, *So, this is where Joe Louis fights...I can do something important, too.... These kids are all bigger than I am.... I'll have to do my very best.*

Then the runners were called to assemble. "Will all the finalists from each of the boroughs please come forward?" an official announced. There was one other black girl in the group. She was from The Bronx. "Runners...take your places.... On your mark.... Get, set.... Go!" the official said.

53

Sitting high in a balcony, Mama, Martha and Willie were oblivious to people sitting next to them. They were busy yelling, "Go, girl. Go!"

Mary didn't feel her feet under her. She felt only a soft wind pushing against her face. Her inner voice spoke to her feet directly. *Run faster, run faster,* it said. She was hot and out of breath as she touched the tape. She barely heard the judge's voice announcing the winner, her heart was pounding so loudly in her ears.

"The winner of the 40-yard dash is—Mary DeSaussure!"

As she approached the official to receive her medal, she looked into the white man's eyes and at his broad smile. He was the same official who had presented her with the silver medal at the Armory. He put the box holding the medal into her hand, and closed her fingers over it. "See," he said, as he looked into her eyes, "I told you that you could win over here!"

Clutching the gold medal to her chest, Mary looked out at the spectators, hoping to see Mama smiling with approval. But there were too many people moving around. She looked down again at the medal and turned it over in the box. *It's really mine,* she thought. *This time the judging was fair.*

Mama, Martha and Willie made their way through the crowd to Mary. They were excited and wanted to see the medal. Mary proudly placed the precious box into Mama's hands. She couldn't smile any deeper when Mama said, "That's my girl. That's my Mary!"

and enfolded her in her arms. Martha and Willie hugged her on top of Mama's hug.

CHAPTER 9

Propelled by a champion's excitement, Mary jumped up and down and around in a circle with Martha and Willie. Suddenly, they all couldn't wait to get home and show the medal to Daddy. Mama was radiant with her joy for her child, too. Her little girl had bested everyone. "God is good, God is just," she said quietly to herself. "My little child showed us all who was best."

Mama knew that opportunities and rewards were not equal for everyone in America. She remembered the racial prejudice she lived with growing up in the South: the signs in public places with bathrooms that said, "Colored Only," segregated schools, and having to ride in the back of the public bus. As a girl, she read the Bible, and tried to make sense of her world in its pages. She found spiritual comfort in believing that God watched over everyone; that He knew where everyone was at all times; that He would make sure each person ultimately got an equal share of the good and the bad. But God's human creatures on Earth irritated her more than a little, and she found herself mad at the injustice of white man's intolerance. Yet, even in those hurtful times, Mama had complete faith in God. "When He says it's time, it will be time," she said more than once.

Mama thought about New York City and her first years in a mixed neighborhood where Black people and white people had friendships on the job, in school and at home. The mixture of ethnic backgrounds on Gates

Avenue was good. Everybody seemed to have come from somewhere else to make a home and a better life. She now watched her happy little girls and thought, *My little Mary is the first Black child to win this competition, my Mary is a pioneer. My goodness, she is just like Joe Louis! Maybe God is showing us that it is time.* She smiled at her children and said, "It's time, children. We'd best be getting home."

The family walked quickly to the subway and found four adjacent seats in the car. Mary pinned the gold medal to the front of her coat. Mary kept pointing to her medal for people to see it, and talked to nearby passengers who smiled at her. "See what I won. I won the gold medal at The Garden."

Although Mama's heart was one with her daughter's elation, she motioned to her, sternly, to sit down next to her. She leaned over and whispered into Mary's ear, "God has been good to you. Be respectful."

Mary thought that the train would never get to their stop and that she would jump out of her skin before it did. She fairly flew up the steps to their apartment and screamed with happiness as soon as she was through the door. "I won, Daddy. I won!" She danced around Daddy, and he beamed at her. Then she unpinned the medal and handed it to Daddy.

"Praise the Lord, Praise the Lord. You really made it, Mary." Daddy spoke in his strong preacher voice, and sounded like he was proclaiming a truth for all the world to hear. Mary liked the finality of the decree.

❖　❖　❖

On Monday morning, the twins ran their familiar route to PS 129. They'd been going to school there since kindergarten. They looked for Luther, the friendly black patrolman from the 79th Police Precinct, who was their school crossing officer. Everyone loved Luther. Mary wanted to share her news with him before anyone else at the school. Luther was kind, but stern. He knew every child by name. The children respected him for his kindness, and for the power of the Police Department that he represented. Even the rowdies walked a straight line when they were near him. Neighborhood parents were grateful for his after hours concern, too. If Luther saw a child alone after school, he would walk that child home. At Christmas, Luther got a blizzard of presents.

When Luther saw Mary's medal and heard her story, his face filled with a wide smile. "Whoo whee," he sighed. "I'm really proud of you. Really proud, Mary."

Mary flashed him a champion's smile, and then ran to catch up with Martha, who was just joining their special group of friends, the "Rifettes." These girls usually walked to school together, stayed together at recess and walked home together. Some girls not in the group called after them, "Here come the River Rats." Today, Mary didn't care about differences. Everyone with ears was the same to her. She told everyone in the Rifettes, everyone in her class, and her teachers, about the race and winning the gold medal...which she promptly showed off.

❖　　❖　　❖

Mary's mouth calmed down in a couple of days, and life went back to normal. The medal was put away in her dresser drawer for safe keeping, although she would check on it every day. It was her proof that the race had not been a dream. Sometimes, she'd hold it up to the light to see its warm, golden glow. Sometimes she'd speak to it like a friend. "Wow! You are really something else. Aren't you beautiful. I won you. And you don't care what color I am. Don't you ever leave me, you hear me?!" She would always make sure of two things. First, to return the closed box to her drawer, and second, never to admire the medal when her sisters were around. Not that Mary thought Martha or Willie would ever take it, but she couldn't be sure that if one of them might be jealous, she could decide to play a trick and hide it somewhere else in the apartment.

Mary was right, in a way. There were times when Willie took the medal out to look at it and wished that it were hers. But, feeling guilty for just holding it, she always put it back before Mary or Martha or Mama caught her with it.

Thinking about her sisters' honesty helped Mary discover something about herself that she did not like. Daddy always said, "Remember the Commandment that says 'Thou shalt not steal.' Never take anything from someone without his or her permission." She knew that her sisters wouldn't. But she did! She took Willie's

59

Cuban-heel shoes without asking her permission on the day of the Preliminaries. The shoes got soaked from the rain even though she wore galoshes over them. She'd ruined them. Willie cried all night about her best shoes. Suddenly Mary understood the true meaning of what she did. Raising her eyes toward Heaven she whispered, "God, I promise I will never do anything like that again! Amen!"

Several days after the big race at the Garden, Mr. Jackson again saw the twins at the Sumner Avenue grocery store. He called across the street to Mary, "Little girl, how did you do?"

"I won the gold medal. I did."

Mr. Jackson crossed the street to speak to the girls. "That's wonderful! I didn't see it in the newspapers because the big story was our big push in the war. The American Army crossed the Rhine and our Marines landed on Iwo Jima. Reporters don't give space to a track meet when there's a war to be won and our boys are doing it. Any other day and you'd have been a news feature...with pictures. It would have been a nice newspaper spread for you." Mr. Jackson paused, then added, "Mary, do you want to run again?"

"When? Where? Really?"

"Oh, yeah, I think we can get something going. I'll have to go to the 79th Police Precinct and talk to the captain...see if there's anything in the works...."

"Oh, first you'll have to talk to my parents."

"Of course." Mr. Jackson nodded. "You have other friends. Would you like to start a track team the way the German-American girls did? Bring your friends to play at the Sumner Avenue Playground, too."

This time Mary caught herself before answering. "You'll have to ask my parents. I couldn't tell you yes or no. You'll have to come to my home."

Later, Mary quietly enlisted Martha and two girls from the Rifettes for the team. Martha always knew she could run as fast as Mary, and she had been wanting a little of the spotlight, too. Since she had always done things with Mary, she felt sure that this was right, part of God's plan. Willie was not interested. She had more responsibilities helping Mama around the house, and going with her to redeem the family's government coupons for clothes and food at the Armory on Pennsylvania Avenue. Sometimes they would spend hours waiting in line to pick up things like baloney, sheets and children's clothing. The clothing was all identical, but Willie's and Mama's magic fingers would alter the designs just enough to give the pieces a little individuality. Willie also enjoyed more of a private life than the twins. She was not a spitfire sports girl, and she didn't like to look messy. In fact, she was a cool and calm perfectionist. She always looked perfect, her clothing was always where it was supposed to be, and so were her toys.

No, joining the running team was not for her, but she would loudly cheer them on. Mary decided not to tell Mama and Daddy about her recruitment activities until after Mr. Jackson had a chance to talk to them.

Mr. Jackson visited the 79th Police Precinct three times, and had long talks with Captain Vincent Kiernan, about future PAL track meets that his new team could enter. A meet was planned for McCarren Park, and Mr. Jackson's girls were eligible! Now it was up to the girls, and up to their parents to consent. He would break the news to the group at the playground on Saturday. The group was playing there regularly.

Mary immediately said, "I do want to run, Mr. Jackson, but you'll have to speak to my parents."

"Wonderful. I'll walk home with you and Martha later today."

Daddy's eyebrows showed his surprise at seeing Mr. Jackson at his door again. Once Mr. Jackson explained the reason for his visit, the two men had a long and serious conversation. Mama sat quietly nearby. Mr. Jackson began by saying that PAL, the Police Athletic League, ran the track meet. The races had the support of the New York City Police Department.

Daddy, who had great respect for the law, immediately decided that the endeavor must be legitimate, but he asked about responsibility for the girls, "Who looks after them? And I want details, young man!"

62

Mr. Jackson explained how he, himself, would be in charge. He went on to tell Daddy that the meet could open doors for the girls that otherwise would remain closed to Negroes.

Daddy looked at Mama for a long moment, then solemnly declared, "Mr. Jackson, I will put you in charge of my daughters, but you make sure that nothing interferes with their school work. It comes first. This running thing is not a necessity." Then Daddy gave his blessing to the new endeavor.

Mama sat thinking about her girls. *Willie never gives me any trouble, but the two spitfires could be a handful. They rarely think about the reactions that their impulsive acts could bring.... They already fill the house with their friends and noise.... What will it be like now?*

Mr. Jackson was thinking about the permission forms he had to get from each of the other girls' parents.

Captain Kiernan lost no time in making the first black PAL sanctioned girls' track team a reality. As soon as all the girls' paperwork was in order, he promptly assigned two coaches to the team—Mr. Jackson and Mr. Willliam Mosner, a white Jewish officer.

The team ran against other Brooklyn teams in McCarren Park. Only Mary had a real gymsuit, everyone else on the team wore shorts, t-shirts and sneakers. They looked different from each other, but they all shared the experience of being on a real team.

63

Mary won a gold medal in the 40-yard dash, and Martha won a silver in the 50-yard dash. From this time on, the twins were on their way to stardom ...together.

Above: McCarren Park, spring of 1945. 79th Precinct first track meet. Martha is center front.

Below: McCarren Park, 1946. 79th Precinct Team Trophy presentation, Brooklyn Champs. Left to right: Patrolman Mosner, Mr. Jackson, Reggie Batson, Harry Wills.

64

CHAPTER 10

The new Stuyvesant Heights Girl's Track Team proved itself. The girls were the talk of the 79th Police Precinct, and the twins were the heart of the team as it rolled on to win borough and city-wide meets. The team was a unit in spirit and purpose. All the girls held hands in silent prayer before each meet. And Willie was always on the sidelines cheering the girls on. Martha showed that she had tremendous energy and power. She became a stronger and technically better runner than Mary. Mary was happy that they were sharing the adventure and that they could practice and gossip together.

Coach Mosner became a good friend to the girls, and a part of the team. Blond, tall and thin, he was handsome in his uniform. With an easy smile, he made sure that his girls were never hungry and that their stamina was high. He treated them to hot dogs and ice cream. He kept morale high. But, the day he told them that he'd have a surprise after the meet, his voice sounded somehow sad, and the girls were unnerved. They did not do well in the races that day, feeling somehow that his news would not be good. They gathered around him to hear his news.

"I am sorry to tell you that I can no longer be your coach," he began.

"Oh, no! What did we do wrong? We'll practice harder, longer. We love you. Don't leave us...please don't!" They all spoke at once and tears streamed down their cheeks. They wrapped their arms around him. It was a while before they gave him a chance to continue speaking.

"Oh, girls, I'm not leaving because you're bad. I'm leaving for a good reason. I'm getting married."

The children gasped with surprise, then pleaded, "Even if you do get married, can't you still have some time with us? Show us a picture of your fiancée." The young woman in the picture was very pretty, yet the girls felt that she was their enemy, and they pouted.

"Now wait a minute. Stop those long faces," Patrolman Mosner said. "Even if I'm not here, this team will continue. I already spoke to Captain Kiernan and he has appointed Patrolman Americo Bacci as my replacement."

The girls sighed in relief and sadness. Then they lined up to shake Patrolman Mosner's hand and wish him good luck. Tears trickled down their faces and they said between sniffling, "Don't forget to come see us run when you can."

Patrolman Mosner waited until each girl was picked up by her family, then when the area was empty, he adjusted his cap and walked away.

It didn't take the girls long to discover that Patrolman Bacci was as nice and caring as Coach Mosner. An Italian-American, Coach Bacci looked nothing like

66

Coach Mosner. He was shorter, and rather stocky. His hair was dark brown and his complexion was swarthy. He had a warm smile and an easy laugh. The girls felt as though they were part of his family, because he spent many "after hours" with them.

Once, after a successful meet, Coach Bacci treated the whole team to the Coney Island Amusement Park. It was here that they tasted pizza for the first time, and loved it. Only Mary hung back, saying, "No, no, no, I'm not going to eat that gooey mess."

The whole team and Coach Bacci had to coax out her bravery before she very slowly took a tiny bite of the tip of the cheesy slice. A larger bite was followed by Mary's broad smile. "Another pizza lover for life!" they yelled, and doubled-over laughing.

CHAPTER 11

As the weeks slipped on, Mary and Martha continued to win medals. Their classmates at PS 129 raptly listened to stories they told about their meets, their friendships with the patrolmen, the places they went and the fun they were having. Some were eager to join the team, and did. Others just listened to the stories and wished they had the girls' ability and popularity.

The fall of 1946 brought change; graduation from PS 129 and going to high school. Daddy and Mama thought that Girls High School would be perfect for the twins. It had an excellent educational reputation, a good ethnic mix of students, was a safe school, and there would be no boys to take the girls' minds off their studies. Willie was already there, and doing well.

The evening before the girls' first day in Girls High, they overheard Daddy and Mama talking about their running success and their future. Daddy was proud of them, and trusted in the Lord's way. His girls were good. Mama, although happy for their success, was more pensive. "B," she said, "Willie's almost all grown, and now Mary and Martha are going to high school. Will they be able to handle all the pressure? I mean the racing meets, the publicity, the awards and newspaper people swelling their heads. And how about their popularity? Will they be able to resist vanity? They have to be good in school to make something of themselves. Coach Jackson has kept them busy and away from troubled kids, and Coach Bacci really makes them feel good about themselves. But, do you think all this running can help them get a college education? I dream about that for them B. ...B?"

But Daddy's rolling snore told her he had long ago fallen asleep.

In Girls High School, Mary and Martha were programmed into the same classes. One of their favorite teachers was Miss Sarah Delaney, their English teacher. She was the most sophisticated, well-groomed lady they had ever met. Her straight, graying hair was pulled back, her clothing was simple and immaculate. Her posture was perfect, and silver-framed glasses set off her lively dark eyes. Miss Delaney was a no-nonsense teacher, yet she had a sense of humor. Mary and Martha and many of her other students thought that she was white and Jewish. Years later they were surprised to learn of her African heritage. Miss Delaney never tried to "pass." Because of her fair skin, nobody ever thought her to be anything but white.

Miss Delaney was a stickler for neatness. Books had to be flat on desks, and homework had to follow her format precisely. Not a thing missed her scrutiny.

Martha was the class devil and full of mischief. One day she wanted to get a reaction from Miss Delaney and see how long it would take the teacher to spot what was different in the classroom. She placed a piece of crushed mincemeat pie from a Christmas party in

69

another class on top of an empty desk, and waited. Miss Delaney moved up and down the aisles of her classroom, checking on her students' work. She stopped at the pie's desk, raised an eyebrow, then scrunched her face in disgust. Moving toward her own desk in the front of the room, she said, "What is that?! Martha, get that thing out of here immediately!" She removed several sheets of brown paper toweling from a drawer and held them out to Martha. Dutifully, Martha wrapped the objectionable blob in the towels and threw the package into the waste-paper basket. She was hot with embarrassment. Miss Delaney had called her name to clean up the mess without a second thought, and her classmates were covering their mouths to stifle their laughter. *My clowning days are over,* Martha thought. *It won't be funny if Miss Delaney reports me to the principal as a trouble-maker.*

Miss Delaney sometimes sipped from a silver, purse-sized flask during class. Some of the girls winked at each other and said, "Miss Delaney's at her gin again." The twins hid their smiles, too. But many years later they were both relieved to read that Miss Delaney's "gin" was most probably an herbal mixture. She and her sister, Bessie, wrote in their autobiography, *Having Our Say,* that they were extremely health conscious and they were herbalists.

Miss Delaney wanted her girls to grow up and find success in life. She taught English well, but she instilled self-esteem and was a model of dignity by example. Mary and Martha gained perspective from her and

70

decided that although running was important, a college education and degree were their long-term goals.

Martha and Mary on graduation day from
P.S. 129, June, 1946.

71

CHAPTER 12

Mary and Martha ran, and the team roster grew as schoolmates and neighborhood friends joined. Now, the team needed an official name. The girls chose "Trail Blazers." And so it passed into history that New York City established its first official PAL African-American Girls' Track Team, the Trail Blazers. The year was 1947.

The Trail Blazers' colors were to be black and white, with the green and white PAL patch proudly displayed. Serious fundraising had to be done for uniforms, and neighborhood families joined the effort through raffles, cake sales and fundraising parties. This was a busy and happy time.

Church picnics in Van Cortlandt Park in The Bronx gave Mary and Martha an opportunity to watch experienced runners on the cross-country trails. They wanted to learn; to practice more efficiently. They followed in the runner's paths. Even in the summer's heat, they ran up and down the thousand steps in the park. They ran everywhere to keep building their muscles and endurance. They begged their coaches for a more regularized training routine. They wanted an assigned place and time for all the girls to practice. They dreamed of winning gold medals, and they were not afraid of the work and commitment championship

72

would take. Finally, Coaches Bacci and Jackson had good news. Doc Ellstein of Boys High School agreed to let the Trail Blazers practice in the 13th Regiment Armory for an hour after his training session ended. Combined with their natural abilities and what they learned from watching the boys, the Trail Blazers flourished and became a winning team at city-wide meets.

Mary's heart was filled with joy because God had allowed her to play a large part in starting the team.

| Betty | Mary | Mary |
| Hermann | Ballard | DeSaussure |

Betty was given the victory, but Mary's foot is clearly over the finish line before Betty reached it. See next page.

73

74

1946. Indoor track meet, Bedford Avenue Armory, Brooklyn, New York. Martha is victorious.

CHAPTER 13

Being a Trail Blazer brought out different emotions in each of the DeSaussures.

Mary came out of her introvert's shell and showed her feelings. She showed anger when she didn't win, or when she made a mistake, and she had been known to fly into a jealous rage when others received praise and she felt she was overlooked. Because she became so vocal, some of the girls started calling her "the evil twin."

A bad time for Mary came one day during a relay race at the Bedford Armory when she lost her concentration and dropped the baton. The Trail Blazers had to forfeit the meet and give up their chance to win the PAL Golden Track Shoes and Sweatsuits Awards. Teammates were furious at her. Another bad time was more personal. To maintain her light weight for the starting position on the "B" Team and in the 40-yard dash, she put herself on a strict diet of milk and pretzels, until her body began to rebel and she realized that her stamina and health were suffering.

Martha was heavier and stronger than Mary. She was the "A" Team starter. Calm, smiling and friendly, she was dubbed "the good twin." She could easily run 50, even 100-yard dashes.

Willie, at the sidelines, loudly cheered the team on. When fans identified her as "Mary and Martha's big

76

sister," she felt proud. And she was quick to smile when members from the other team would yell at her, "Ya don't hafta cheer. Those DeSaussures are gonna win anyhow!"

The New York City *Amsterdam News* carried in-depth stories about the team. Its ace reporter, Mr. Jackie Reems, told Coach Jackson, "I'm recording these events for history." *The Daily News, The New York Times, The Herald Tribune, The Brooklyn Eagle, The Police Gazette* and *The Journal American* also carried articles and pictures about the Trail Blazers. The growing rivalry between Mary and other teams' stars like Betty Hermann and May Faggs made high interest stories and sold papers. (May Faggs went on to compete in the 1952 Olympics.)

In 1947, Coaches Jackson and Bacci wanted to make the Trail Blazers part of the PSAL, the Public School Athletic League, which up until now had been open only to boys. It would be a model for the school system. They presented their idea to the New York City Board of Education. It was rejected.

Meanwhile, Mary and Martha joined the PAL black Drum and Bugle Corps at Wynn Center in Brooklyn. Mary played the xylophone. Martha was a baton twirler. Wynn Center was a magnet for kids like Floyd Patterson, who later became a champion boxer, and Benjamin Ward, who later became Police Commissioner of New York City. Mr. Norwell Clark was the center's director, Samuel Austin developed the Drum and Bugle Corps, and Joe Tucker was drill/instrument instructor.

The twins were having fun. And once again, they were poised to become part of "firsts" for Blacks.

By all accounts, their Drum and Bugle Corps was the first black-American PAL band ever invited to march in the New York City St. Patrick's Day Parade. It was also the first to perform at a home New York Giants football game. And an outstanding first was taking shape behind the scenes with the Trail Blazers.

PAL officials Police Commissioner John Brennan and Jack Reid were planning more prestigious meets and an organizational change. The best runners from all the PAL centers, including the German Athletic Track Club, were to be grouped into a single team. This team would be officially registered with the AAU (Amateur Athletic Union) and would be able to compete throughout New York State and on the inter-state circuit. The new team would be the first integrated track team in the history of New York City representing PAL. Patrolmen Jackson and Bacci were relieved of their coaching positions, and the name Trail Blazers was retired.

In 1948, the twins and other members of the PAL team were invited to participate in the Millrose Games in Madison Square Garden. They were also invited to join the Olympic Development Program. The invitation was an honor extended only to top athletes, and Mary and Martha seemed on their way to the 1948 Olympics in London, England.

But tragedy struck at home. Daddy was diagnosed as having terminal cancer, and all thoughts and prayers were with him. Even as the girls made the bus trip to the Olympic tryouts at Brown University in Providence, Rhode Island, their hearts were with him.

The weather was dismal. Their tears mixed with the raindrops on their faces. Mary was entered in the 100-yard dash, a race she'd never run before, and at the starter's gun, she ran off the field in tears. Her coach was furious. Martha managed to place in her 100-yard dash qualifier.

Daddy slipped closer to death as the next Olympics eliminations were scheduled. The trials were to be at Randall's Island. Mama didn't want the girls to go. They begged her. The bus waited. Finally, after a long silence, Mama said, "Yes," very quietly. But by then, the bus had left without them.

Sad, yet stubborn and determined, Mary and Martha ran to the "A" subway train and took it to 125th Street in Manhattan. From there they ran across the bridge to Randall's Island. They heard the roar of the crowd cheering on the field. They willed their feet to fly. And Martha prayed, "Please don't let my race be over." But her event had started, and the girls were already in motion. She begged the officials to let her run against the clock. "Please, let me run for time. I know I can do it. I'm fast. Please..." But her request was denied. Sobbing, she ran to Mary. Both girls were devastated.

Daddy died a few weeks later. The girls' world had come apart. Mama remained in deep mourning long after they buried Daddy in his hometown in South Carolina.

In 1950, Mary and Martha graduated from high school. Their interest in running seemed to have faded along with their dreams of glory. There would be no Olympics or college scholarships. They felt that there were only memories of what once was, and what could have been.

The First Team of the P.A.L.'s American Girl Track Team

The article appeared in the *Police Gazette* in 1948.

P.A.L. GIRLS SWEEP METROPOLITAN AAU MEET

FIFTEEN GIRLS of the P.A.L. running in the Metropolitan A.A.U. opening track meet of the season at the 22nd Regiment Armory against several of the country's greatest women track athletes, swept the two women's events in a history-making debut by taking the first five places in the 75 yard dash, running with six yard handicaps in a field of 40 entrants, and in the 440 yard relay by running away with first, second and third places against leading club teams of the metropolitan area.

As a result of this fine showing, the Police Athletic League has been invited to enter a special invitation 440 yard relay race for girls at the Millrose games January 31 at Madison Square Garden. They will run against four other team selected by officials of the German-American A.C. of New York and others.

Although the P.A.L. girls are only 15 and 16 years of age, A.A.U. officials expressed the belief that they will make a fine showing in the National Championships and are looked upon as possible Olympic entrants.

In the 75 yard dash, the girls finished as follows:

1. Mae Faggs, 15, 111th Pct.
2. Martha Dessassure, 15, 79th Pct.
3. Dorothy Klein, 16, 62nd Pct.
4. Mary Taylor, 15, 79th Pct.
5. Gloria Moett, 15, 79th Pct.
Time: 0:08.4 sec.

80

79th Pct. Poster Contest, 1947. Right side: Capt Kiernan,
Patrolman Bacci, Mary in stripped shirt.

81

COMMISSIONER WALLANDER is shown in the photo presenting the Police Commissioner's Trophy to the captain of the 79th Pct. P.A.L. Track team, winner of the third annual indoor track championship of the Police Athletic League.

Left to right: Capt. Vincent J. Kiernan, Mary Dessanssure, 50-yard dash winner; Billy Christiansen, 880-yard run winner; Dorothy Middleton, 40-yard dash; Al Trumpet, team captain; William Jackson, coach, Commissioner Wallander, Kenneth Francis, 40-yard dash, and Dep. Commissioner James B. Nolan, president of the P.A.L.

The 79th Pct. team, over a hundred strong, won the third annual city-wide indoor track championships with a team score of 46 points, beating out the Thomas Wynn P.A.L. Center, which was second with 28 points. The meet marked the culmination of the winter track season of the P.A.L. It was preceded by five borough meets from which the best runners entered the city-wide finals, which were run off at the 23rd Regiment Armory, Brooklyn, on Lincoln's Birthday. Over 7,000 youngsters, both boys and girls, participated.

Eighteen precincts and P.A.L. centers scored points in the meet. In third place was the 105th Pct., Queens, with 20 points, followed by the Young P.A.L. center, 12 points; 66th Pct., 11 points; 34th Pct., 10, and the 111th, 40th and 62nd Pcts., 8 points each.

There were sixteen events in all, four of them for girls. The 79th Pct. also won the Brooklyn Borough Meet, and last summer took the outdoor trophy.

Presentation of the Police Commissioner's Trophy to 79th Pct. PAL track team, 1947. Far left: Capt. Vincent Kiernan and Mary, who won the 40 yard dash.

82

79th Pct Track Team at City Hall, 1947. Capt. Kiernan receives Mayor's Trophy from Mayor O'Dwyer. Mary and Martha third from left, first and second rows.

Wynn Center Drum & Bugle Corps marching in New York City's St. Patrick's Day Parade, 1947.

83

Martha as a member of the Drum & Bugle Corps at Wynn Center in Brooklyn, New York.

Color Guard of Wynn Center Drum & Bugle Corps, Rosalee, drum majorette. 1947.

84

Mary and Martha, Coney Island, 1950.

85

CHAPTER 14

Mary and Martha knew that they were intelligent, leaders, strong-willed, and God-fearing. They were determined to achieve success in other fields. They did.

Today, Mary and Martha are leaders in their own interest areas. Both rose in the ranks of the Women's Auxiliary of the National Baptist Convention; VARANA, the Volta Region Association of North America; and the Women's Africa Committee of the African American Institute. Mary retired recently from the Elmhurst Hospital Center as Administrative Executive Secretary to the Director. Martha became the *first* Black Aministrative Secretary in the New York Supreme Court in Brooklyn, and then the *first* Black Legal Administrative Secretary to work in the Appellate Division. She has been a team with Justice William C. Thompson—the *first* Black judge in the Appellate Court of Kings County—for more than thirty years. When she graduated from John Jay College of Criminal Justice with a B.S., she did it with an award for excellence in academic achievement. Both of the women have firecracker personalities that light up any room they are in. Both are loving mothers.

PAL had opened doors for them that changed their lives, and PAL had given them the self-esteem to believe in themselves as leaders in their social world. Both young women gave thanks for their own running ability and PAL's opportunities, and vowed to give back the

86

gift of opportunity and empowerment to other youths when they could. They have.

In 1973 Mary, along with Patrick Hartwell and Morris Singleton, graduates of Boys High School, formed a youth's track club, The Queens Trail Blazers. Mr. Fred Thompson, Meet Director of the Colgate Games, gave financial support to the team. Mary recruited girls from parks and playgrounds. The jumprope crowd and the double-dutchers were good prospects. She'd ask them, "Do you want to learn to run, to meet people, to grow?" She wanted to expose the youngsters to another level of living. "A rose could blossom, with a little nurturing," she said. For a decade Mary remained active in The Queens Trailblazers. She also was a member of the William J. Ramos Track Club. She is still involved with PAL activities.

During the 1970's, Mary and Martha were among the organizers of the William J. Ramos Track Club which sponsored track and field events for young boys and girls throughout the boroughs.

Top: First Marty Ramos Track Team, 1973. First standing row center: Robert Moss, to his right, Shirley Chisholm, to her right, James Gathers and Mary.

1973 - Martha at a School In - The 41st Assembly District Brooklyn, with the late speaker of the Assembly, The Hon. Stanley Steingut.

88

Colgate-Palmolive Company
300 Park Avenue
New York, N.Y. 10022

DAVID R. FOSTER
PRESIDENT AND
CHIEF EXECUTIVE OFFICER

Mr. Pat Hartwell   March 3, 1975
Queens Trail Blazers

Dear Mr. Hartwell:

We at Colgate-Palmolive have been most gratified by the outstanding
success of our first Colgate Women's Games.

In particular, it has been an inspiration for me personally to
witness the spirit and enthusiasm of all these young women competitors over the past several months.

Additionally, it was most satisfying to learn from the many parents
of these competitors, who took the time to write and thank us for
our efforts in helping to bring recognition to these young people.

We acknowledge that you and your track club are responsible for
keeping the entire concept in women's track and field alive, by
your work with them throughout the year.

For this unselfish giving of your personal time, we wish to recog-
nize you and your contribution to women's track and field in general,
as well as to the Colgate Women's Games.

As a token of our appreciation, please accept the enclosed $1,000
check with our sincere thanks and continued best wishes.

We are looking forward to next year and to working with you and
your splendid competitors in the 2nd Colgate Women's Games.

                              Sincerely,

                              David R. Foster
                              President

DRF:ro
Enc.

89

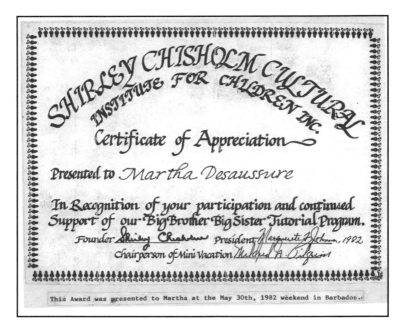

SHIRLEY CHISHOLM CULTURAL INSTITUTE FOR CHILDREN INC.

Certificate of Appreciation

Presented to *Martha Desaussure*

In Recognition of your participation and continued Support of our "Big Brother Big Sister Tutorial Program.

Founder *Shirley Chisholm* President *Marguerite Johnson*, 1982

Chairperson of Mini Vacation *Mildred A. Pilgrim*

This Award was presented to Martha at the May 30th, 1982 weekend in Barbados.

100 BLACK MEN, INC. EDUCATIONAL MEETING AT MEDGAR EVERS COLLEGE, April 24, 1984. L. to R. : Justice William Bellard; Mrs. Martha De Saussure, Executive Secretary to A. D. William Thompson, Justice; Justice Lewis Douglas; Dr. Irene Impellizzeri, Dean of Education, Brooklyn College and Brooklyn Member of the Board of Education; Judge Jerome Kaye; Dara C Johnson, daughter of Professor Sheila Johnson; Presiding Justice Milton Mollen, Appellate Division; Dr. Betty Shabazz, Medgar Evers Public Relation Director; Dean Charles Baron; Borough President Howard Golden; College President Jay C. Chunn.

90

April 29, 1994, Martha with Mrs. Sandy F. Ray leaving the National Secretaries Week Luncheon, sponsored by the Lung Association.

Honoring Indispensable Secretaries

Who's a whiz at the word processor, the typewriter, the FAX machine, the copier and the coffeemaker?

Who saves you from pesky telephone calls? Who is indispensable to you?

Every boss who has a secretary knows the answer to those questions and many customarily show their appreciation by sending bouquets of roses or taking his or her secretary to lunch once a year.

But believing they deserve more, for the past four years the Brooklyn Lung Association has sponsored "Salute to Secretaries," a special recognition on Professional Secretaries Day (Wednesday) for those many agree are largely unsung office heroines and heroes.

This year the association invited the Brooklyn business and professional communities to pay tribute to secretaries and administrative assistants by nominating someone for the group to honor.

The seven women selected will be feted at a luncheon in the Palm House of the Brooklyn Botanic Garden. Among them are: Shelly Blue, executive secretary at National Westminister Bank; Jamie Brown, acting secretary to the vice president, Consolidated Edison; Martha Benton DeSausure, legal secretary to Judge William C. Thompson, a Justice of the Second Department of the State Supreme Court's Appellate Division.

Also: Christine Hunter, executive assistant to the president and chief executive officer of Advanced Technological Solutions, Inc.; Olga Martinez, community relations coordinator, Independence Savings Bank; Diane Nieves, secretary and office man-

Merle English

ager at Harborside Management Corp., and Joyce Smith, executive assistant at Brookdale Hospital Medical Center.

All are happy in their jobs. Thirty years with the same boss attests to that for DeSausure.

The East Flatbush resident, a court employee since 1976, started working for Judge Thompson when he was a lawyer in the Court Street firm of Thomson and Bursley and continued with him through his changing roles as district leader for the 56th Assembly District, city councilman, state senator and finally as a judge.

They are a team.

"He's an excellent boss," she said. ". . . He has a lot of energy and I have a lot of energy. There was a time I had the entire directory of anything he needed in my head."

Like all of the secretaries, DeSausure speaks highly of her boss. Her enjoyment of her work appears to be based on mutual respect, admiration and concern.

"He is a very compassionate man," she said. "He's a great orator, and he encouraged me with my schooling."

DeSausure, a former medal-winning athlete who was a member of the tryout team for the 1948 Olympics in Helsinki, holds an associate degree in legal studies from New York City Technical College and will graduate from John Jay College of Criminal Justice with a bachelor's degree in legal studies in June.

She's a member of the Supreme Court Secretaries Association and is also active in church work as a member of Cornerstone Baptist Church and secretary to the first vice president of the National

Baptist Convention's Women's Convention. Her two daughters are also secretaries to judges in the Supreme Court.

She has two grandchildren.

"She's fabulous," said Judge Thompson, father of former Deputy Borough President Bill Thompson. "Without her I'm dead."

The judge remarked on his secretary's loyalty, a quality for which Frank J. Maddalena, Brookdale Hospital's president and chief executive officer, salutes his executive assistant, Joyce Smith.

"Her calm efficiency and warm, friendly manner has graced the executive suite for the past 26 years," he wrote in her nomination letter. "I have been impressed with and deeply grateful for her perseverance, dedication, knowledge and loyalty to the hospital and the communities we serve."

Like DeSausure, Smith, also a grandmother, is active in many civic and social organizations. She serves on several committees of Bridge Street A.W.M.E. Church and bowls in a weekly league.

DeSausure, speaking for secretaries everywhere, commented, "Sometimes the public believes a secretary is just there, but a secretary to me is truly professional. If she enjoys her job, she tries to make everything great for her boss."

As it hosts the borough's official tribute to its secretaries, the Brooklyn Lung Association seeks to help fight lung disease.

Employers of honorees help defray the cost of the luncheon. And proceeds from a raffle and congratulatory messages and advertisements in a journal published for the occasion help fund the association's educational activities.

Tickets to the event cost $60 and may be obtained by calling (718) 624-8531.

CHAPTER 15

In preparation for *Running Against the Wind,* Mary and Martha sat down with their biographer, Inge, and created the following time-line of their running careers. As they listed each event, they alternately laughed and cried and hugged and high-fived. They agreed over and over again, "It was a great run!"

1945

New York City Department of Parks "Olympic Carnival Track Meet" Preliminary—Brooklyn, New York 13th Regiment Armory. Mary is given silver medal for 40-yard dash.

New York City Department of Parks "Olympic Carnival" Borough-wide Track Meet—Madison Square Garden, New York City. March. Mary won Gold Medal for the 40-yard dash.

Mary recruited Martha and some friends to join in forming the first PAL team to run for the 79th Precinct: Mary Ballard, Dolores Walks, Dorothy Middleton, Ruth Brighthaupt, Helen Platts and Ruby McMahon.

First PAL local track meet—McCarren Park, Brooklyn, New York. Mary won the 40-yard dash and Martha took second place in the 50-yard dash.

1946

Recruited Vivian Carr, Susie Wade, Gloria Moett, Sarah Jones, Janice Harris and Edna Brown to run for the PAL team. The name "Trail Blazers" was chosen for the team after the recruitment of new members.

"PAL Third Annual City-Wide Indoor Championship Track Meet"—Bedford Armory, Brooklyn, NY. Mary won the 40-yard dash, Martha the 50-yard dash. The Girls' Relay team took first place in the 440-yard relay. The 79th Precinct won the Indoor Title.

"PAL Brooklyn Borough Outdoor Trophy Track Meet"—McCarren Park, Brooklyn, New York. Mary won the 50-yard dash, Martha the 60- yard dash. The Girls' Relay Team won the 440-yard relay. The 79th Precinct won the Outdoor Title.

1947

First PAL African American Drum and Bugle Corps to march in St. Patrick's Day Parade in Manhattan, and to march for the Giants football game at Yankee Stadium. Mary and Martha were members.

PSAL—PAL coaches made an appointment to appeal to the New York City Board of Education to establish PSAL for girls, using the Trail Blazers Track Team as the subject. After discussion, the idea of having PSAL for girls was rejected.

Trail Blazers PAL Track Team's name retired. The new team would be called "Police Athletic League, AAU Track Team." Consisted of teams A and B which were made up of the best runners from the PAL precincts in each borough. Merger allowed the new team to enter the more prestigious track meets with a more challenging field of athletes. Martha starter for "A" Team. Mary starter for "B" Team.

Millrose Games—Mary and Martha members of the women's PAL Team invited to participate at the games to be held at Madison Square Garden in Manhattan, New York.

Knights of Columbus Track Meet—Jamaica Avenue Armory, Queens, New York. Martha started for Team "A." Mary started for Team "B."

Metropolitan AAU Track Meet—Madison Square Garden, Manhattan, New York. Martha started for "A" Team. Mary started for "B" Team, with a handicap.

Olympic Developmental Track Meets—168th Street Armory, Manhattan, New York. Mary and Martha participated in this training.

93

1948

Mary and Martha participated in the Olympic Tryouts—Brown University, Providence, Rhode Island.

Olympic Qualifying Meet—Randall's Island, New York. Mary and Martha arrive too late to participate due to the critical condition of father. Meet had started and officials would not allow Martha to run for time.

Father passed away.

1949

Martha and Mary ran in PAL Regional Track Meets.

1950

Mary and Martha graduated from Girls High School in Brooklyn, New York, and ended their track careers.

CHAPTER 16

Although the Police Athletic League, PAL, has been a friend to the youth of New York City for more than 80 years, the history of the organization is not generally known.

The agency which has helped so many youngsters transcend family and neighborhood barriers began in 1914, when Police Commissioner Arthur Woods, who was genuinely interested in the city's poor, became actively concerned about the children who lived in the overcrowded tenements with no safe places to play. To improve their situation, he ordered a city-wide search for vacant lots which would be turned into playgrounds. He also set aside twenty-nine blocks to become playground blocks. They would be closed to traffic in the afternoons every day except Sunday.

The New York Times reported that, "Children must play, and children, if they live in cities, must play in the streets." The reason for creating playground blocks was two-fold; first, to "reduce the temptations of wrongdoing by keeping children off the streets and by giving them a chance for wholesome play under proper supervision," and second, "to reduce tensions between police officers and youth."

Public reaction to Commissioner Woods' New York City playstreets plan was extremely favorable. Later when he inspected these playstreets, mothers personally

95

thanked him, and children waved at him with their thanks.

During the same time that Commissioner Woods opened the first playstreets, Captain John Sweeney of a Lower East Side precinct formed the Junior Police. His was a more organized recreational program for boys, ages eleven through sixteen. They dressed in police uniforms, took part in marching drills, and carried green and white flags that predated PAL's future banner colors. The purpose of the Junior Police was to promote a more cordial relationship with the police, and to uphold the values of good American citizens. The organization was modeled after the Police Department hierarchy. Boys were first inducted as patrolmen and promoted up the ranks to chief inspectors. Meetings were held twice a week. The boys participated in marching drills, track meets and baseball games. Members enjoyed public swimming pools, learned first aid and personal hygiene.

By 1917, the Junior Police expanded into thirty-two precincts. When Captain Sweeney retired from the police department, the Junior Police was dissolved. The idea of an organized recreational program for New York City's poor children would not surface again for ten years!

However, the playstreet programs continued. With the cooperation of New York City's Traffic Commissioner and the Mayor's Committee on Recreation and Playgrounds, by 1924 seventy-five more playstreets were created in Manhattan, Brooklyn, the Bronx, and Queens.

The Crime Prevention Advisory Committee, focusing on juvenile delinquency, was appointed by Police Commissioner Grover A. Whalen in 1929. The theory was that "a trouble-making boy today would become a hardened criminal tomorrow." In 1931, the Police Department got involved in providing recreation for New York City's youth to try to curb future crime. Mayor James J. Walker signed a bill that made the Crime Prevention Bureau a permanent part of the Police Department.

1931 also marked the year that the Twilight Baseball League was formed by a Crime Prevention officer. This league consisted of eight baseball teams for young boys. The entire community came to the financial aid of the league, and materials and labor were donated to build a baseball field with bleachers. The Twilight Baseball League grew in popularity, and basketball and football were added. The expanded league became known as the Twilight Athletic League.

"During a Depression," the Annual Report of the Police Department warned, "it is the children who stand in the greatest danger of permanent injury." To counteract this danger, the Crime Prevention Bureau formed the Junior Police Athletic League in 1932. This new institution was an outgrowth of the Twilight Athletic League, and a committee was formed to oversee it. It was headed by baseball legend Babe Ruth, Police Commissioner Edward Mulrooney, and Deputy Commissioner of the Crime Prevention Bureau, Henrietta Addition. The main focus was baseball, but boys also received boxing instruction and played football. The first girls' basketball teams were also formed.

By 1936, The Police Athletic League was reorganized. Junior membership cost ten cents, and adults were recruited as associate members at one dollar each. Police Commisioner Lewis J. Valentine obtained a list of five thousand truants from the New York City Board of Education. He hoped to enroll them in PAL programs.

To celebrate the new organization, the first week in August was declared "PAL Week." A carnival was held in Union Square, where children competed for prizes. Former Governor Alfred E. Smith and Boxer Jack Dempsey released five thousand balloons from the Empire State Building. Each balloon carried a coupon redeemable for Junior membership. A boxing match in Staten Island marked the beginning of the PAL's involvement with the borough of Richmond.

The nation was suffering a terrible depression, and President Franklin D. Roosevelt's WPA helped the PAL in important ways. By 1937, seven hundred and fifty workers from his newly created WPA (Works Progress Administration) were assigned to help the PAL.

The PAL membership grew to 70,000 in the late 1930's because of the support of the WPA staff. There were sixty-nine indoor centers, many of which were dedicated to the memory of police officers who died in the line of duty. Recreational activities increased and now included arts, crafts, aquatics, dancing, theater, kindergarten, motion pictures, nature study trips, special events, games and sports. Various radio stations included weekly educational programs featuring PAL staff and children.

The Fox Lair estate in Warren County, New York, was leased to the Police Athletic League in 1938. It became a camp and gave 120 underprivileged boys an opportunity to have a month of vacation in fresh air and sunshine.

In 1939, PAL played an important part at the World's Fair in New York City. September 6, 1939 was declared "PAL Day." More than two thousand members participated in sports and cultural activities. A complete playstreet was set up in the center of the fair to display the PAL's programs.

Aggressive fundraising was needed for PAL to survive, so the PAL held a benefit at Madison Square Garden in 1939. It was called "Stars Shine for Young America," and it raised $25,000. Many famous stars, including Rita Hayworth, helped to make the benefit a success.

By 1942, there were no longer WPA workers at PAL, and there were rumors of cutting the budget for the Juvenile Aid Bureau because of dwindling funds during the war. But a public outcry to save the PAL was successful, and funds were found for its continuance.

PAL children aided in the war effort by organizing scrap salvage drives, and helping with Red Cross and

Civil Defense activities. They promoted the sale of war bonds, and collected fats and waste paper. PAL provided supervised care for the children whose parents were involved in war work and civil defense duties. PAL worked to keep morale high on the home front.

After World War II ended, PAL expanded. The Eleanor Roosevelt Field was opened in 1945, and Mrs. Roosevelt threw out the first baseball. Fox Lair Camp —closed during 1944 and 1945—reopened in 1946. That same year, Mayor William O'Dwyer began a campaign to stop juvenile delinquency, and pledged, "one hundred percent support" to PAL. Trained social workers were hired to help treat emotionally troubled children.

During the 1950's PAL-trained boxers captured the Golden Gloves title. PAL athletes also competed in the Helsinki Summer Olympics in Finland in 1952, and in the Melbourne Olympics in Australia in 1956.

The 1960's saw an expansion of PAL's educational programs. The Head-Start pre-school program was begun in 1964. PAL libraries opened with a focus on Black and Puerto Rican history. And PAL began an annual Brotherhood essay contest, choral group performances, and added neighborhood playmobile vans.

During the 1970's, PAL expanded futher and participated in nation-wide youth programs designed to educate young people about the dangers of drug abuse.

100

In the 1980's, PAL reached out again, this time to disabled children by providing a horseback riding program.

In the 1990's, PAL has been changing to satisfy the needs of New York City's youth. It approaches the millenium with enthusiasm for the future of kids and young adults. Today PAL's program areas include Youth Centers, Educational Programs, Special Programs Concerning Drug Abuse and Graffiti, Citywide Art & Writing Contests, Summer Programs, Employment Training and Placement, Precinct Programs and Sporting Leagues.

PAL continues to be a beginning for many young people throughout the City...kids just like Mary and Martha.

John J. Ryan, Executive Director of PAL
and Mayor Rudolph Giuliani, 1995.

102

John J. Ryan, Executive Director of PAL, Robert Morgenthau, Chairman of PAL, and Benjamin Ward, Commissioner (Ret.) of N.Y.C. Police Department, 1995.

80th Anniversary celebration of PAL, 1995, at New York City Police Headquarters. Left to right: Martha, Jeannette Gadson (Deputy Borough President, Brooklyn), & Inge Auerbacher.

104

The DeSaussure sisters, 1999

105

Appendix A: Song Lyrics & Music

Running Against The Wind

Words by Inge Auerbacher
Music by James Donenfeld

Despite all odds my star will rise,
Above the clouds and to the skies.
Have a little faith in me,
'Cause I can do it, you will see.

Refrain:

See, I'm trying, and I'm flying,
Let the race begin.
I'll be ready, I can win,
I'm running against the wind.

Oh, I will soar to heights unknown,
My dream is real and mine alone.
I will start today and begin,
If I believe then I can win.

Repeat refrain

Please don't slow me down, I'll get my crown.
Now I have the force, I'm right on course.
This is the hour, I have the pow'r,
I'm coming through, this is my cue.

There's danger on the road ahead,
But, by my spirit I'll be lead.
With each step the victory is mine,
My goal's in sight, and I'm doing fine.

Repeat refrain

Copyright © 1997 Auerbacher and Donenfeld

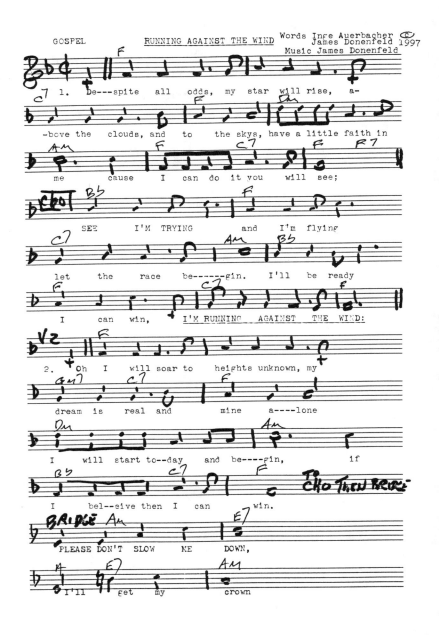

1. De---spite all odds, my star will rise, a-
-bove the clouds, and to the skys, have a little faith in
me cause I can do it you will see;
SEE I'M TRYING and I'm flying
let the race be------gin. I'll be ready
I can win, I'M RUNNING AGAINST THE WIND:
2. Oh I will soar to heights unknown, my
dream is real and mine a----lone
I will start to--day and be----gin, if
I bel--eive then I can win.
BRIDGE
PLEASE DON'T SLOW ME DOWN,
I'll get my crown

108

page 2 (running against the wind) ©1997 J.Donenfeld

now I have the force

I'm right on course

this is the hour I have the power

I'm comming through, this is my cue;

3. There's danger on the road a--head, but

by my spirit I'll be led,

with each step the victo----ry is mine, my goal's in

sight and I'm doing fine.

SEE I'M TRYING AND I'M FLYING

let the race be-------gin; Oh

I'll be ready I can win, I'M

RUNNING A----GAINST THE WIND.(end).

109

Appendix B:
Ethnic and 1940's Period Recipes

Graham Pudding Dessert

Serves 5 to 7

Ingredients:

2 boxes Jello chocolate pudding

1 box Nabisco Graham Crackers

4 cups whole milk

½ teaspoon vanilla extract

½ stick butter

½ cup sugar (optional)

1 glass baking dish–either square or 9"x12" rectangle

Pour contents of chocolate pudding boxes into a saucepan adding the milk, butter, vanilla and sugar. Cook over medium heat, stirring mixture continuously to make it smooth. When mixture begins to boil and thicken and bubbles appear, remove from stove and place aside. Pudding will continue to thicken as it cools.

Prepare glass baking dish. Place a layer of Nabisco Graham Crackers in the bottom of the dish. Spoon in some of the pudding mixture so that the crackers are fully covered. Add second layer of crackers, covering pudding as evenly as possible. Cover with pudding mixture. Place third layer of crackers. Set aside until the bottom of the dish has cooled (approx. 20-25 mins.). Refrigerate until ready to serve.

Options: Can be served with a non-dairy topping or whipped cream.

Note: This recipe was made by Mrs. Hattie DeSaussure on special occaisions, or when the girls requested it for Sunday dessert.

Lasagna

Ingredients:

1lb. lasagna noodles, boiled

sauce:

1 green pepper, sliced thin

2 medium onions, sliced thin

2 tbsp. olive oil

1 kernel garlic, sliced thin

1 No. 2 can tomatoes

½ cup water

1 small can tomato paste

1 tsp. salt

1 lb. chopped beef

cheese:

2 cups (16 oz.) mozarella cheese, shredded

4 cups (32 oz) ricotta cheese

3 tbsp. grated parmesan cheese

Brown onions and green pepper in 1 tbsp. of olive oil. Add garlic, tomato paste, tomatoes and water. Bring to a boil. Put aside. Heat 1 tbsp. olive oil and add meat. Add salt. Brown. Drain. Add meat to onions and other vegetables. Simmer for 15 mins. stirring occasionally.

Boil the lasagna noodles in a large, flat pot until soft. Make the sauce. Assemble in a 9"x12" baking dish in layers with the cheese the following way: Cover the bottom of the dish with lasagna noodles, cover the noodles with some mozarella and ricotta cheese, cover the cheese with sauce. Repeat, ending with a layer of meat sauce and cheese. Sprinkle on parmesan cheese.

111

Cover dish with foil and bake for ½ hour at 375º. Remove foil and bake 5 mins. longer. Remove from heat and allow to stand for several minutes.

Option: Serve with salad made from Victory Garden lettuce, tomatoes and cucumbers, and Mrs. DeSaussure's pound cake for dessert.

Fried Chicken

Ingredients:

1 cup flour

1 koshered (heavily salted the previous night) fryer chicken

1 cup flour

salt to taste

pepper to taste

Crisco shortening

Prepare chicken:

Singe off any fine hair feathers. Wash salt off thoroughly with water. Pat dry. Cut up into frying pieces—drumsticks, thighs, wings. Cut breast into two halves, then in half again.

Put flour in mixing bowl together with salt and pepper. Dip chicken in mixture. Fry in deep fat at 375º until well-browned on both sides,

Place in dripping pan and cover. Fry for 10 mins. Then remove cover to crisp for 5 mins. more.

Options: Serve with collard greens and potato salad.

113

Chicken Stew

Ingredients:

¼ slice salt pork

2-3 tbsp. flour

2 large onions, sliced

4 celery stalks

1 large bell pepper, coarsely chopped

1 3-4lb. stewing chicken, cut up into small parts–feet, drumsticks, thighs, wings, neck, breast (cut into at least 4 pieces)

2 full cups water

dash of red pepper

dash of black pepper

salt to taste

a large stew pot

To prepare:

Singe off any fine hair feathers, wash thoroughly, pat dry and set aside. Place salt pork in the bottom of pot. Cook over medium heat to extract drippings. Remove and set aside. Add flour and onions to the drippings and brown to medium color. Add the water to the mixture and salt to taste. Cover pot and bring broth to a boil. Lower flame and add chicken, salt pork, celery, green pepper and seasonings. Let chicken simmer for 1 hour or until soft.

Options: Serve with collard greens from Victory Garden and boiled rice and Graham Pudding Dessert.

114

Plain Cake–Hand Mixed

Ingredients:

6 eggs, at room temp.

2 cups sugar

3 sticks butter, lightly salted, at room temp.

4 cups all-purpose flour

4 tsp. baking powder

1 cup milk, at room temp.

4 tsp. lemon extract

1 large pan, greased

1 large mixing bowl

1 pot (to melt butter in)

Preheat oven to 350º. Melt butter and let cool. Set aside. In large bowl, sift 4 cups of flour and 4 tsp. of baking powder. Sift mixture again, then set aside. Separate eggs, put yolks into one bowl and whites into another. Beat the yolks for 2 mins. (if using a mixer "blend" for 1 min.). Now add the sugar and melted, cooled butter and lemon extract. Mix until fluffy. Next add flour, a cup at a time alternating with a little of the milk, and mix well. Beat egg whites until they slightly peak, them fold them into the batter. Pour batter into greased pan and bake at 350º for 1 hour or until toothpick inserted into center comes out clean.

Tips:

1. You can use any extract of your choice for flavoring.

2. Wrap cake in cheesecloth when it comes out of the oven while still warm.

3. Let the pan cool for about 20 minutes before the cake is taken out.

Gefilte Fish

Ingredients:

Use $^2/_3$ whitefish and $^1/_3$ pike

to each pound of fish use:

1 egg; separate yolks and whites; beat whites

1 tsp. matzo meal

1 tbsp. cold water

1 small onion

¼ tsp. sugar

salt and pepper to taste

1 large stewing pot with cover

Put fish that has been skinned and boned through a meat grinder. Chop onions in a wooden bowl. Add fish, egg yolks and other ingredients (except egg whites) to onions. Chop thoroughly. Fold in beaten egg whites. Shape mixture into elongated, one inch thick patties, oval shaped.

Cut enough onions to fill bottom of large stew pot. Place fish bones on top of onions. Lay fish patties on top of fish bones. Just cover with cold water. Cover pot.

Cook on low flame to simmer for 2 hours.

Remove fish patties. Strain broth and set aside to gel.

Option: Serve fish patties with grated horseradish.

116

Appendix C: PAL LOCATIONS IN NEW YORK CITY

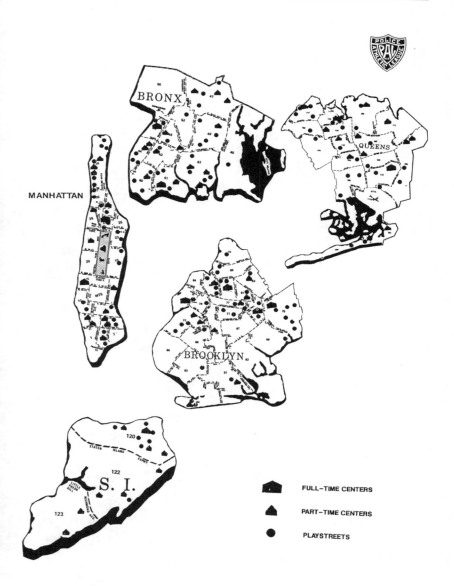

FULL-TIME CENTERS

PART-TIME CENTERS

PLAYSTREETS

117